American Journeys

WEEKENDS ACROSS THE U.S.

American Journeys
WEEKENDS ACROSS THE U.S.

EDITED BY JOHN M. THOMPSON

NATIONAL GEOGRAPHIC

WASHINGTON, D.C.

CONTENTS

Foreword: American Journeys 8

Pacific Meditations 10

Mountain Views & Desert Vistas 38

The Old Frontier 66

North Country Expeditions 90

Southern Secrets 118

Yankee Landscapes 146

Appendix: Further Journeys
176

Acknowledgments & Credits
188

Index
189

PREVIOUS PAGES: Kayaking the Intracoastal Waterway near Beaufort, North Carolina;
The Natchez Trace Parkway carves a path of history through the South.
OPPOSITE: Music is always just around the corner in New Orleans, Louisiana.

Str. of Georgia

Str. of Juan de Fuca

Orcas I.

Port Townsend

Olympic N.P.

Puget Sound

Seattle
WASHINGTON

Mt. Rainier
14,411

Mt.
St. Helens
8,366

Astoria

Lewis and Clark N.H.P.
Cape Lookout S.P.

Mt. Adams
12,307

Portland

Yaquina Head
Newport

Columbia

Columbia River
Gorge N.S.A

OREGON

Malheur
N.W.R.

Burns
Crane

Hart Mt. National
Antelope Refuge

Hart Mt.
8,018

Steens
Mt.

CHAPTER 1
WEST COAST

Mendocino

Placerville

San Francisco

American R.

Santa Cruz
Monterey Bay

Monterey

Carmel-by-the-Sea

Monterey Bay
National Marine
Sanctuary

CALIFORNIA

Sierra

Nevada

GREAT

NEVADA

BASIN

Great Salt
Lake

UTAH

Death Valley

−282

Mojave

Desert

Colorado City

Las Vegas

CHAPTER 2
WEST

Glen Canyon
N.R.A.

Grand Staircase-
Escalante N.M.

Bryce Canyon N.P.

Lake
Powell

Fredonia

Pipe Spring
N.M.

Grand
Canyon
N.P.

Flagstaff

ARIZONA

Zuni

Zuni
Mts.

Los Angeles

Palm
Springs

Joshua
Tree N.P.

Anza-Borrego
Desert S.P.

San Diego

Salton
Sea

Colorado

Sonoran

Desert

Phoenix

Tucson

Santa Rita
Mts.

Tombstone
Patagonia

Pacific

Ocean

ROCKY

CANADA

MONTANA

Missouri

Butte

Big Hole National Battlefield

Virginia City

Bannack

Bitterroot Range

IDAHO

Continental
Divide

WYOMING

GREAT

Fort Berthold
I.R.

Lake Sakakawea

Audubon N.

Fort Mandan H.S.

Washburn

Cross Ranch

Fort Clark S.H.S.

Bismarck

NORTH DAKOTA

Bighorn Mts.

Sheridan

SOUTH DAKOTA

De Sm

Vernal

Dinosaur
N.M.

Colorado

Mt. Elbert
14,333

Buena Vista

Black Canyon
of the Gunnison
N.P.

Sangre de Cristo Mts.

Boulder

Denver

Fremont Pass

Leadville

Pikes Pk.
14,110

Salida

COLORADO

Taos

Santa Fe

Albuquerque

Acoma
Pueblo

NEW MEXICO

P L A I N S

Platte

NEBRASKA

Arkansas

Tallgrass Prairie
National Preserve

KANSAS

R O C K Y   M O U N T A I N S

OKLA

CHAPTER 4
CENTRAL SOUTH

TEXAS

Edwards

Plateau

Rio Grande

Aust

San
Antonio

San Antonio
Mission
N.H.P.

SELECTED FEATURES

●● City or town

▫ Point of interest

+ Elevation (in feet)

········ National Marine Sanctuary

▫ National Park Service

▫ National Forest Service

▫ State Park

▫ Indian Reservation

▫ National Wildlife Area

MEXICO

AMERICAN JOURNEYS

CHAPTER 6
NORTHEAST

CHAPTER 3
MIDWEST

CHAPTER 5
SOUTHEAST

CANADA

Lake Superior

Bemidji
Lake Itasca
Itasca S.P.

MINNESOTA

Minneapolis
St. Paul

Sioux Falls

Omaha

IOWA

Amana
Des Moines

Mississippi

WISCONSIN

Ephraim
Green Bay

Milwaukee

Galena
Mississippi Palisades S.P.

Chicago

ILLINOIS

Indianapolis

INDIANA

Columbus

MICHIGAN

Lake Michigan

Mackinac I.

Lake Huron

Detroit

Lake Erie Islands

Lake Erie

Cleveland

Berlin

OHIO

Columbus

Ohio

Lake Ontario

Buffalo

PA.

Pittsburgh

Johnstown

Laurel Highlands
Fort Necessity
Nat. Battlefield

Seneca Rocks
Monongahela
N.F.

W. VA.

Lewisburg

Lexington
Berea

KENTUCKY

Tennessee

TENNESSEE

Memphis

Mississippi

ARKANSAS

Little Rock

Eureka Springs

Ozark Plateau

Neosho

Tulsa

Guthrie

Oklahoma City

Abilene
Topeka
Council Grove
Strong City
Cottonwood Falls
Cassoday
Flint Hills

MISSOURI

Katy Trail S.P.
Hermann
Augusta
St. Louis

Dallas
Jefferson
Kilgore
Caddo Lake S.P.

Lufkin

Big Thicket
National Preserve
Beaumont
Houston

LA.

White Castle
Baton Rouge
Sorrento
Garyville
New Orleans

Jackson

MISSISSIPPI

ALABAMA

Birmingham

Columbus

GEORGIA

Atlanta

Okefenokee
Swamp

Lake
Seminole

Apalachicola R.

Apalachicola

FLORIDA

Jacksonville

Cumberland Island

Tampa

Miami
Coral Gables

Florida Keys

Straits of Florida

Gulf of Mexico

CUBA

Mt. Katahdin 5,268
Mt. Kineo 1,789
Moosehead Lake

ME.

Mt. Washington 6,288

Adirondack
Park
Adirondack
Mts.

VT. Hanover
N.H.

MASS. Boston
Lenox
Stockbridge
The Berkshires
Providence
R.I.
Cuttyhunk Island

Cape Cod

NEW YORK

Cold Spring

CONN

Long Island

New York

Bucks County

New Hope
NEW JERSEY
Doylestown

Philadelphia

MD.

Bridgeton

Delaware Bay

DELAWARE

Washington, D.C.

Richmond

VIRGINIA

Chesapeake Bay

Abingdon
Johnson City
Jonesborough

Raleigh

NORTH CAROLINA

Asheville
Charlotte

Beaufort

Pamlico Sound

Cape Lookout

SOUTH
CAROLINA

Columbia

APPALACHIAN MOUNTAINS

Atlantic

Ocean

miles
0   500

kilometers
0   500

American

The 48 contiguous states are so packed with great destinations that even with a narrow focus, a traveler still has many choices to make. In the mood for northeastern mountains? The Laurel Highlands, the Adirondacks, and Maine's Mount Katahdin are but a few of the possibilities. How about cities in the south-central United States? New Orleans and San Antonio both spring to mind. In fact, every region has plenty of its own wonderful cities, small towns, and outdoor treasures. That's why this book is loaded with mini-journeys: brief profiles of some of America's favorite vacation spots.

We've designed each journey specifically with the weekend traveler in mind. Whether you have a few days off from a business trip, or you just need to get away for some quick rejuvenation, or you simply want to dream about what's out there—these snapshots of great places to visit in the United States are intended to get you going.

Plenty of classic American destinations fill these pages. There is nowhere in the world like Las Vegas for around-the-clock high-gloss fun. And everybody has to see Chicago's soaring skyline—it would be downright un-American not to. The great painted deserts of the Southwest, the wave-crashed coastline of Oregon, Lewis and Clark's wild North Dakota, and the literary Berkshire hills are all must-see standards of United States tourism.

Alongside these, though, we've chosen several lesser known places, hidden away from the mainstream of American life. The Flint Hills of Kansas have a lot to offer that's not

Journeys

apparent on a quick drive through; the Apalachicola Coast is so unheralded that few people stop, thus missing a wonderfully undeveloped stretch of Florida. Likewise, Jonesborough, Tennessee; Cutchogue, New York; and Berlin, Ohio: They are little dots on the map, but they are destinations well worth a few days of any traveler's time.

Imagine that for just one weekend your only task is to discover what special things a place has to offer. There are no set agendas. You can do everything—or nothing. And, in the pursuit of relaxation, you never know what will unfold.

You may chance upon a beautiful old rocking chair in a wayside antique store in Doylestown, Pennsylvania, or dine by candlelight in a creaky 18th-century tavern in Abingdon, Virginia. You could be tapping your toes to the rambunctious strains of an oompah band in Hermann, Missouri; watching a scarlet sun slip into glimmering waters off Mackinac Island, Michigan; eating homemade fruit pies in the Amana Colonies of Iowa; hiking to the top of a 14,000-foot peak in Colorado; or eating fresh Pacific oysters in a dockside restaurant near Monterey, California. On another weekend you could be listening to B. B. King on a Memphis blues outing or sipping a cocktail during an art deco tour of Miami.

The possibilities go on. We hope that the American journeys we have outlined in this book will start you dreaming, scheming, and enjoying your weekend adventures. ≈

Chapter 1

Pacific Meditations

California coastal icon: A lone cypress clings to a rocky outcrop at Pebble Beach on Monterey Bay,

THE WEST COAST

The most striking thing about America's West Coast is its infinite variety. What this means for those seeking the perfect weekend getaway is that "perfect" can be defined in any number of ways. From the Olympian peaks of Washington and the wave-lashed coast of Oregon, to the port cities and backcountry deserts of California, the region abounds in unending wonders, all possibilities for journeys, whether natural or historical.

Journeys to this far edge of the North American continent seem always to offer the thrill of discovery. Take, for example, the charming seaside village of Port Townsend. Its frontier-era buildings on the rocky coastline of the Strait of Juan de Fuca stand just north of Olympic National Park, a majestic wilderness of glacier-crowned mountains and old-growth forests in Washington's Olympic Peninsula. Going from town to park, or vice versa, you can feel as if you have come across something entirely new. A similar sense of

PREVIOUS PAGE: Lupine, Indian paintbrush, and other wildflowers carpet a meadow in Mount Rainier National Park. Visible from 200 miles away, Mount Rainier looms large in the lore and geography of the Northwest.

discovery awaits just inland in the spectacular volcano country between Seattle and Portland. With the landscape ever changing, particularly at Mount St. Helens, there is always something new to see.

Just west of Portland, the northwest coast of Oregon appears made for two- and three-day jaunts. Delightful seaside villages punctuate a running series of coastal state parks, where high bluffs drop to rock-strewn beaches. Whales migrate along here, and year-round seabirds populate the sheer cliffs. Farther south, the Monterey Bay area offers a different angle on the Pacific Coast—modish communities vie for attention with coves brimful of dazzling marine life.

Nautical Days

Perched on the northeast corner of the Olympic Peninsula, Port Townsend is one of the most delightful little towns on the West Coast. Full of charm and easy-going sophistication, this historic seaport

wafts visitors back to an era when schooners and steamers carried schemers and dreamers to the virgin lands of the Pacific Northwest.

Port Townsend rises up from the sheltered waters of Port Townsend Bay to a series of high bluffs that overlook Admiralty Inlet, a passageway into Puget Sound. Ferry boats, yachts, and sea kayaks have replaced the multimasted schooners that once dropped anchor here, but the town still marinates in the glow of its rich maritime past.

As proud residents like to point out, Port Townsend was founded in 1851, six months before Seattle. A customs center, it was the area's most important commercial maritime nexus and quickly became the busiest harbor on the West Coast. But Port Townsend's boom turned into a big-time bust in 1893, the year an eagerly anticipated transcontinental railroad failed to arrive, having been routed to Seattle instead.

Ironically, economic disaster saved Port Townsend for posterity. There wasn't enough money to tear down old buildings or build new ones, and so the fabric of the 19th-century seaport has hardly changed. Restoration efforts were bolstered in the 1970s when the lower waterfront area and upper residential neighborhoods were deemed national historic districts. Since that time, to the delight of architecture buffs and old-house enthusiasts, the entire town has undergone a virtual retro-renaissance back to its Victorian roots.

PORT TOWNSEND

Port Townsend is generally mild all year round and at its sunny best in summer and fall. The Port Townsend Visitor Information Center (2437 E. Sims Way; 360-385-2722 or 888-365-6978; www.ptguide.com) provides a free driving tour map that highlights the town's Victorian architecture and maritime-related culture.

Sailboats line the marina at Port Townsend, Washington, a mid-1800s seaport that preserves its charm into the 21st century. Attractive architecture and grand views of the Cascades, the Olympic Mountains, and Admiralty Inlet make this Puget Sound gem a delightful weekend escape.

The waterfront area, where the regular passenger ferry from Whidbey Island chugs in and out of its small terminal, is a perfect place to begin. Water and Washington Streets, running parallel to the harbor, are chockablock with redbrick commercial and civic buildings erected over a century ago, when Port Townsend was the official port of entry to the northwestern United States. The sailors, immigrants, and brawling adventurers who once jammed these streets would be bewildered by the galleries, coffee shops, and fine restaurants found here today.

Sitting in the rain shadow of the grandiose Olympic Mountains, the town receives only a fraction of the precipitation that drenches Seattle. And with the area's mild temperatures, people here tend to be outdoors-oriented.

Festivities often take place at the north end of town in Fort Worden State Park. Built in the late 1890s to protect against sea invasion, the fort was used through World War II but never saw military action. The former bastion is now a serene park with views across sparkling Puget Sound.

Up in smoke: A billowing column of ash and smoke rose 60,000 feet into the atmosphere when Mount St. Helens erupted on May 18, 1980. The blast killed 57 people in the sparsely settled area.

PREVIOUS PAGES: *Point Wilson Lighthouse stands proudly in Washington's Fort Worden State Park in Port Townsend. The 49-foot octagonal tower dates from 1914; its light was automated in 1976.*

Volcano Trail

From magma flows in ancient times to 20th-century eruptions, volcanoes have sculpted the Pacific Northwest's dramatic topography. The so-called Volcano Trail steers visitors northeast from Portland into southern Washington, down sinewy forest roads that link a trio of peaks and delve into a world of lava beds, canyons, and caves. Some of the sights are well known, others less so—but all showcase volcanic wonders.

The third highest of the volcanoes in the Cascades, 12,307-foot Mount Adams dominates the skyline northeast of Portland. Without the pyramid summit that characterizes many volcanoes, the humpbacked mountain became known as the "forgotten giant"—misidentified by Lewis and Clark, shortchanged by cartographers (who understated its elevation by 3,000 feet for decades!), and still overlooked by many outdoor enthusiasts.

On May 18, 1980, climbers on Mount Adams saw an amazing sight. Some 35 miles west, a lateral blast from deep within the Earth shattered the north face of Mount St. Helens. Ten minutes later a heat wave swept over the climbers, raising the air temperature 30° to 40° F. The blast pulverized the top 1,300 feet of Mt. St. Helens and triggered 1,600° pyroclastic flows, instantly rearranging more than 200 square miles of landscape. A mushroom cloud of ash billowed more than a dozen miles into the sky. People as far away as Canada and Montana heard the explosion.

Today, 110,000-acre Mount St. Helens National Volcanic Monument protects the truncated mountain and its scarred surroundings. The nearby Johnston Ridge Observatory offers fantastic views of the gaping crater that was left when the peak collapsed. Park roads course through a scoured landscape that today is only beginning to return to life. In the fall of 2004, park visitors were treated to proof of the volcano's active status when plumes of steam and ash spewed from the mountain, continuing for the next few months.

To the north, the undisputed king of the Cascade volcanoes, tallest of all at 14,411 feet, Mount Rainier dominates the vistas of western Washington. Native Americans called it Tahoma—great snowy mountain—a name befitting a peak with more than 35 square miles of glaciers. In 1792 explorer George Vancouver renamed it for Rear Adm. Peter Rainier, a British naval officer who never saw the mountain himself. Any number of native peoples, pioneers, climbers, painters, and sightseers, though, have been awed by the grandly towering, snow-topped volcano.

The U. S. Congress proclaimed Mount Rainier and vicinity a national park in 1899. But the mountain's real genesis dates back about half a million years. Molten rock erupting from a weak spot in the Earth's crust started the process. Over time, sluggish lava flows and further eruptions built up the composite volcano until about 6,000 years ago, when it is thought to have reached a height of 16,000 feet above sea level.

Another major eruption occurred 2,500 years ago, creating a second volcanic cone at the summit; several minor eruptions shook the mountain around 1840. Today Mount Rainier is still a work in progress, perennially prone to an occasional mudflow or exhalation of steam and ash. Indeed, scientists are certain that Mount Rainier will erupt again, although they are unable to predict when.

VOLCANO TRAIL

Best months to explore the Volcano Trail are June through September. Wildflowers usually peak in early August, autumn colors in late September. Snow closes many Forest Service and Park Service roads from November to late May. Contact the Gifford Pinchot National Forest (10600 N.E. 51st Circle, Vancouver, WA 98682; 360-891-5000; www.fs.fed.us/gpnf); Mount Adams Ranger Station (2455 Hwy. 141, Trout Lake, WA 98650; 509-395-3400); Mount St. Helens Visitor Center (3029 Spirit Lake Hwy., Castle Rock, WA 98611; 360-274-2100); or Mount Rainier National Park (Tahoma Woods, Star Route, Ashford, WA 98304; 360-569-2211; ww.nps.gov/mora).

PREVIOUS PAGES: *Before and after—visitors compare a picture of magnificent Mount St. Helens to the current view from Johnston Ridge Observatory, only five miles from the crater.*

A spectacular road runs nearly 20 miles from the park's southwest entrance along the forested banks of the Nisqually River, then corkscrews up to the glorious Paradise Valley, where subalpine meadows are backed by an awesome view of Mount Rainier. This postcard-perfect valley lives up to the hyperbole, especially in July and August when wildflowers bloom. A six-mile stretch of the Wonderland Trail passes 168-foot-high Narada Falls before emerging in the valley—truly the best way to reach Paradise.

Down to the Sea

With its crashing surf, towering headlands, and seal-studded coves, Oregon's central and northern coast is a wild wonder to behold. Whether hiking through a rain forest high above the Pacific or strolling a white stretch of beach sprinkled with sand dollars, visitors discover that the uncrowded Oregon coast lets them get up close and personal with nature on a very grand scale.

SEASIDE OREGON

The weather on the Oregon coast is unpredictable, but summer and fall are your best bets for mild, clear (or at least rainless) days. Contact the Oregon Tourism Commission (775 Summer St. N.E., Salem, OR 07301; 800-547-7842; www.traveloregon.com) or Oregon State Parks (800-551-6949; www.oregonstateparks.org).

Taking a walk along the picturesque bayfront in Newport, one is likely to hear barking sea lions. This lively fishing town on Yaquina Bay is home to the Oregon Coast Aquarium, which provides an introduction to the creatures and eco-systems along the Pacific. Visitors can walk inside an acrylic tunnel that snakes through ocean habitats and offers living displays of sharks, rays, and thousands of other fish. Special tanks hold graceful jellies, seahorses, and dozens of other deep-dwelling denizens.

Just north, at the Yaquina Head Outstanding Natural Area, the gleaming white column of Oregon's tallest lighthouse, built in 1873, presides over a scene of rugged offshore islands teeming with murres, oystercatchers, cormorants, puffins, guillemots, and gulls. Harbor seals laze on rocky ledges and slide into the wave-tossed sea.

North about 50 miles, the coastal highway swerves inland to avoid a series of three capes. So much the better for those who want to get off the main thoroughfare and glimpse some of the most spectacular shoreline on the West Coast. The 39-mile Three Capes Scenic Drive loops past dairy farms, spruce forests, small villages, and majestic coastal headlands. Visitors should take the time to explore on foot via an easy trail at Cape Lookout State Park, which winds high above the sea, through old-growth rain forest with moss-draped Sitka spruce and western hemlock to breathtaking views at the cape's end.

The farthest point south Lewis and Clark traveled on the Pacific coast is now the quaint town of Seaside, the oldest and largest ocean resort in Oregon.

The scenic drive continues inland, through lushly green coastal valleys dotted with grazing herds of Holsteins, Jerseys, and Guernseys. It rejoins the main highway at Tillamook, headquarters for Oregon's dairy industry. This county churns out some 55 million pounds of cheese each year. At the Tillamook County Creamery Association, you can watch the process.

In Oregon's northwest corner, the Lewis and Clark National Historical Park commemorates the explorers' 1805-06 winter camp. They spent a miserable winter here, waterlogged, flea-bitten, hungry, and bored. They suffered from colds, rheumatism, and venereal disease. At least they had made it all the way across the continent to the Pacific coast, an unprecedented scientific and military expedition. As soon as the weather eased up, they turned east and headed home.

Clustered on the mouth of the mighty Columbia River, the town of Astoria came into being not long after Lewis and Clark had departed, making it the oldest permanent settlement in Oregon. Starting as a fur trading post in 1811, the town grew into a thriving port for fishing and logging by mid-century. By the late 1800s some 40 canneries operated on Astoria's waterfront. Though they are gone and

Trappers called the area Malheur, French for "misfortune," but today's Malheur National Wildlife Refuge is considered a prime oasis in southwestern Oregon's desert. The 187,000-acre refuge attracts the white-faced ibis, sandhill crane, American white pelican, trumpeter swan, and other birds traveling the Pacific Flyway.

logging has slowed down, port activities and commercial fishing keep Astoria hopping. With its picturesque waterfront, old-fashioned downtown, and steep streets filled with Victorian-style houses, the town exerts a nostalgic charm.

The Clatsop Spit defines the northwesternmost point of Oregon. Here at Fort Stevens State Park stands a fort built during the Civil War to guard the mouth of the Columbia River. The park's long sandy beach invites one last oceanside stroll. The century-old wreck of the *Peter Iredale*, its iron ribs sticking up from the sand, is a stark reminder that mariners of yore referred to this treacherous section of coastal edge near the Columbia Bar as the "graveyard of the Pacific." The *Iredale*

was one of the lucky ones, with no loss of life. An observation platform on the end of the spit delivers a memorable view of the magnificent Oregon coast.

High and Dry in Oregon

Surprises abound in southeast Oregon. That such an area even exists in this state is perhaps the biggest surprise. No grand conifer forests and rocky seashores can be found here: instead, sagebrush grasslands, cattle ranches, and pocket towns that belong in a Zane Grey novel. Within this unexpected high desert realm, look for duck-filled marshlands, a mountain ridge nearly 10,000 feet high, and a grazing pronghorn herd.

A 70-mile-long massif, Steens Mountain lies at the heart of Oregon's high desert. On the west it slopes up gently from the sagebrush flats; on the east it rises precipitously, a basalt rampart towering a mile above the plain below. Whether travelers ascend from the west via the loop road or rock-climb up from the east along with the bighorn sheep, they reach the 9,700-foot-high ridge, from which most of southeast Oregon is visible. Across thousands of square miles, the only signs of human occupation are a few widely dispersed ranch buildings. The remoteness unnerves and exhilarates.

People come from all over to watch birds at Malheur National Wildlife Refuge. Surrounded by miles and miles of mostly arid terrain, Malheur's 186,000 acres of lakes, marshes, and wet meadows act as a magnet to birds, especially during the spring and fall migrations. In addition to the expectable golden eagles and western meadowlarks, you'll come across species that seem out of place in the desert—white pelicans, sandpipers, and 29 other species of waterfowl.

Wildlife also is the raison d'être of southeast Oregon's other refuge, the Hart Mountain National Antelope Refuge. Established in 1936 as one in a series of national measures to bring the pronghorn back from near extinction, the refuge harbors a summer herd of about 2,000. Because they're here to breed, it's possible to see gawky pronghorn fawns gamboling about as they learn to run, mainly on the open flats on the refuge's east side.

The eponymous Hart Mountain rises above 8,000 feet, and an imposing fault-block wall almost as long and high marks the refuge's western boundary. The deeply incised terrain offers dramatic rifts to hike, such as De Garmo Canyon. A path winds up along De Garmo Creek, following the lush riparian tangle of alder, willow, aspen, and dogwood, where bighorn sheep and prairie falcons thrive in vertical landscapes.

After seeing so much wildlife and driving back roads that go 100 miles without a gas station, travelers may conclude that humans have no place in southeast Oregon. Not so. Native American people lived in these lands for centuries, and then, in the late 1800s and early 1900s, cattle barons, homesteaders, and Basque sheepherders settled in the area. Artifacts of these times can be seen at the Harney County Historical Museum, a pleasing grandma's attic of a museum in Burns. Travelers can visit other historical sites, such as the Pete French Round Barn State Heritage Site. Pete French was a king among cattle barons; his domination of southeast Oregon ended abruptly in 1897, when a disgruntled homesteader shot him in the head.

High Desert

The best weather in Oregon's high desert occurs in spring, summer, and fall, but other seasonal factors matter, too: The road up the Steens typically is open from mid-July to mid-October; the bugs in Malheur are pretty bad in the spring; and the pronghorn high season runs from June through September. For information, contact the Harney County Chamber of Commerce (18 W. D St., Burns, OR 97720; 541-573-2636; www.harneycounty.com).

In Diamond, the next person to walk into the local café easily could be a cowboy, complete with hat and handlebar moustache. Up in Crane, children attend one of the nation's few public boarding schools; their remote ranch and farm houses make daily travel impractical. Frenchglen serves as something of a regional center, with its store, two-room school, gas station, and small historic hotel, yet its population could fit inside a couple of minivans.

Cacti and Cool Pools

The dry and dusty landscape extending from San Diego's backcountry northward to Palm Springs conceals paradoxical personalities. Although Anza-Borrego Desert State Park appears gritty and stone-faced, it tenderly shelters many animals and plants. The oddly humanlike namesake of Joshua Tree National Park lends the desert unexpected personality. The lush playground of the Palm Springs region boasts irrigated golf courses and thousands of swimming pools in a mysterious, sphinxlike landscape.

SAN DIEGO BACKCOUNTRY

San Diego backcountry temperatures are pleasant in winter and hot in summer. Best time to visit: October to May. Contact the Palm Springs Desert Resorts Convention & Visitors Authority (69-930 Hwy. 111, Ste. 201, Rancho Mirage, CA 92270; 760-770-9000 or 800-967-3767; www.palmspringsUSA.com).

About 40 miles east of San Diego, trees begin to thin out. The roadside is lined with spindly, red-flowered ocotillos and yellow-blossomed yuccas. The only signs of man are occasional telephone poles. You've entered Anza-Borrego State Park, an area nearly the size of Rhode Island. This is a region of pink and yellow badlands, rocky peaks, and eroded canyons. Like the landscape itself, the cactuses seem to have popped right out of a Roadrunner cartoon—especially barrel cactuses that inflate like water balloons to hold precious rainfall. Out here every glistening grain of sand, every twig on a creosote bush stands out in the intense light. The world seems hyperreal.

Soon you begin to look deeper, past the weird shapes and into Earth's geological history book. Along the short Narrows Earth Trail, for instance, you see granitic rocks formed about 100 million years ago. And all over the park are alluvial fans, great sprawls of rocks and sand that spread below mountain flanks where rain has washed down everything loose. At the Borrego Badlands, ragged gullies and ridges were cut by storms and tinted pink, green, and yellow by chemical deposits. The sunset alone is worth the trip.

Head north to Joshua Tree National Park, where two deserts meld. The Colorado Desert (part of the larger Sonoran Desert), rising no more than 3,000 feet above sea level, lies in the park's eastern half and is recognizable by its spiderlike ocotillos. To the west spans the higher, slightly cooler Mojave Desert, characterized by Joshua trees. These twisted, prickly yuccas stand with branching arms upraised, so 19th-century

*Hikers admire views of stark ridges and badlands in Anza-Borrego Desert State Park, sprawling
over the mountains between the Pacific Ocean and the Salton Sea in southern California.*

Purple phacelia blooms, above, around a spiky desert agave in Anza-Borrego Desert State Park.
In nearby Joshua Tree National Park, tucked between the Mojave and Colorado Deserts,
the non-cuddly arms of teddybear cholla, opposite, catch lambent sunlight
in the Cholla Cactus Garden.

The waves are renowned for being gnarly near Santa Cruz, where California surfing began when two Hawaiian princesses arrived in 1886 and had redwood surfboards milled for them.

Mormon pioneers named them after the heaven-supplicating prophet Joshua. Indians used the fiber gathered from the tree's tough leaves to make sandals. Cattle ranchers fenced corrals with its trunks and limbs. Keys View, which encompasses 11,500-foot-high San Gorgonio Mountain and the infamous San Andreas Fault, offers the park's greatest vista.

In the Palm Springs resort area, just west of Joshua Tree National Park, winter temperatures linger in the 70s and statistics tell a tale of leisure: 100 or more golf courses, 600 tennis courts, and 30,000 swimming pools. While all the green fairways and irrigated flowerbeds could wither away, though, the desert's stony mountains and endless sand endure forever.

The Palm Springs Aerial Tramway makes a vertical climb of over a mile, from the desert floor up the side of Mount San Jacinto, from the haunt of rattlesnakes to the realm of deer. At the top there are stunning overviews of wooded peaks, the Coachella Valley, and the Salton Sea, shining 40 miles east.

Just south of downtown Palm Springs lie three canyons inhabited long ago by Indians. Andreas Canyon boasts ancient rock art, Palm Canyon is known for its California fan palms, and wild horses live in less visited Murray Canyon. To visit these canyons is to see three more faces of a desert whose paradoxes and timeless beauty emerge only with study and patience.

Sparkling Crescent

Much of the Monterey Bay coastline looks as it did when seafaring Spaniards first arrived in the 16th century. The very unpacific Pacific, its waters rife with sea lions, seals, and other marine life, breaks against miles of granite. Visitors today easily need a long weekend to explore the bay, from the funky town of Santa Cruz to the old Spanish city of Monterey.

A seaside destination since the 1880s, Santa Cruz is a university town known for surfers, eccentrics, and left-wing politics. The University of California established a campus here in 1965 on some 2,000 acres of ranchland, incorporating 19th-century ranch buildings. The Santa Cruz Boardwalk, an old-time amusement park edging a mile-long beach, offers more than 30 rides, including the 1911 Looff Carousel and the 1924 Giant Dipper, one of the world's oldest wooden roller coasters.

Beach volleyball and ocean swimming are big in summer. Surfers have revered the waves off this coastline for more than a century. One primo spot to watch hotdoggers is Steamer Lane, near Lighthouse Point. It's said to be the birthplace of the wetsuit—a surfer here oiled his clothes to ward off the water's chill, so tradition has it.

No visit to Santa Cruz is complete without some time afloat. These waters belong to the Monterey Bay National Marine Sanctuary, one of the world's richest marine environments and home to sea otters, sea lions, harbor seals, and whales. The sanctuary runs along a quarter of the California coastline, from Cambria to just north of the Golden Gate Bridge. Its diverse habitats include wave-washed beaches, kelp forests, and the Monterey Submarine Canyon, which descends two miles into the oceanic abyss, twice as deep as the Grand Canyon.

Monterey has perched on Monterey Bay's southern edge since the 1700s, when Spaniards established a mission here (later moved to Carmel in 1771). After Mexican independence from Spain in 1821, the settlement blossomed into a vigorous port. At the Monterey State Historic Park, you can tour the Custom House, California's oldest government building.

Across the way, Fisherman's Wharf, built in 1846 and still a working pier, holds a festive array of seafood restaurants and shops. Whale-watching and fishing trips leave from here. Adjacent Cannery Row, overlooking the bay, is a similar jumble of ice creameries, gift shops, and galleries. Known for its sardine canneries in the early 20th century, the town's roughneck character back then was immortalized by Nobel Prize–winner John Steinbeck in his 1945 novel *Cannery Row*.

MONTEREY BAY

Monterey Bay's summer fog can hamper visibility for travelers. The beaches are busiest May to November. Contact the Santa Cruz County Conference & Visitors Council (1211 Ocean St., Santa Cruz, CA 95060; 831-425-1234 or 800-833-3494; www.santacruzca.org; or the Monterey County Convention & Visitors Bureau (401 Camino El Estero, Monterey, CA 93942; 831-657-6400 or 888-221-1010; www.montereyinfo.org).

A California sea otter assumes the belly-up position it uses for eating and resting. Vigorously hunted and nearly extinct by the 1920s, these animals, now protected, have made a comeback.

PREVIOUS PAGES: *Dawn brings molten sky and crimson waters to still-sleeping Monterey. Beneath the bay lies 10,663-foot-deep Monterey Canyon, one of the world's largest underwater gorges.*

But perhaps the most famous Monterey address is the Monterey Bay Aquarium, home to more than 250,000 creatures and plants native to the waters just outside. One of the finest aquariums in the world, it successfully combines gee-whiz thrills with conservation-minded education in a facility brilliantly designed to immerse visitors in various marine environments. Giant tunas, sea turtles, barracudas, and sharks swim past the biggest window on the continent, which looks into the aquarium's one-million-gallon indoor ocean. Twice daily a diver feeds fish in a three-story-tall kelp forest.

It's worth detouring from Monterey to drive to the neighboring artists' community of Carmel along 17-Mile Drive, an old toll road with thrilling views of coves, sea lion rocks, mission-style mansions, and the stately Pebble Beach Golf Links with its world-famous water hazards. The drive presents Monterey Bay at its best, a harmonious mingling of natural and manmade beauty. ✍

Underwater gardening: A diver does maintainence in the Monterey Bay Aquarium's three-story kelp forest. The aquarium sponsors ongoing deep-sea research in Monterey Canyon.

MORE PACIFIC PLUNGES

ORCAS ISLAND

The San Juans, a magic archipelago of rocks, islets, and islands lying in the watery embrace of Puget Sound northwest of Seattle, are home to whales, bald eagles, and a few thousand humans who think they've found paradise on earth. Of the four main islands accessible to visitors, Orcas Island casts the strongest spell.

After an hour's ride from Anacortes, ferries dock at Orcas Village, one of three population centers on 59-square-mile Orcas Island. With a general store, a hotel, and rental shops for sea kayaks and bicycles, the village mostly caters to ferry traffic. As you drive or bicycle north on Orcas Road, the island's charms become immediately apparent. Roads twist and turn through a hilly, compact landscape of forest and pasturelands where water shimmers around every bend and 2,407-foot Mount Constitution rises to the east. You won't find a stoplight anywhere on the island. What with kayaking, hiking, and whale-watching excursions, there is plenty to do to fill up a weekend spent here.

Contact: Eastsound Chamber of Commerce (360-376-2273; www.orcasisland.org).

GOLDEN GATE BRIDGE AT NIGHT

SAN FRANCISCO VIEWS

Built on a hilly peninsula flanked by sea cliffs, San Francisco offers fantastic views in every direction. Some vantages are ideal for picnics or hikes, while some lend themselves to sketching or quiet contemplation. Others are ideal for sipping a cocktail and watching the sun set over the Pacific.

The 360-degree panorama from the east peak of Mount Tamalpais takes in the entire Bay Area. Crowning Telegraph Hill, Coit Tower offers a splendid, maplike perspective that encompasses the bay. At lunchtime from the Cliff House, you can soak in the full grandeur of the glowing colors over Seal Rocks and the Pacific. For sunsets, there's nowhere like the legendary Top of the Mark. Or try the jaw-dropping vistas from the Fairmont Hotel atop Nob Hill. On the

KAYAKING NEAR ORCAS ISLAND

water, ferries and tour boats offer splendid views of the Golden Gate Bridge and Alcatraz, along with other islands.

Contact: San Francisco Convention & Visitors Bureau/Information Center (415-391-2000; www.sfvisitor.org).

MENDOCINO HEADLANDS

MENDOCINO

Like Rip Van Winkle, the town of Mendocino appears to have slumbered for a hundred years and awakened to find itself lost in time. The town is on the National Register of Historic Places. Built on bluffs beside the Pacific Ocean, the northern California town was settled in the 1850s by New Englanders whose white clapboard houses still line the streets. Atop the Masonic Hall, the same carved angel has presided over the town for 150 years. On back streets, wooden water towers stand like exclamation marks, as if to say "Remember the old days!"

Not that there aren't signs of modern life. In the 1960s, after its logging fortunes fell and its walls began sagging, Mendocino transformed itself into an art colony. Hippies arrived, trailing fragrant clouds of patchouli, and the New Age brought some new life. Now resurrected by galleries, tourism, and a protective love of its past,

Mendocino carries the feeling of the 1850s—and the 1960s—into the new millennium.

Contact: Fort Bragg/Mendocino Coast Chamber of Commerce (707-961-6300 or 800-726-2780; www.mendocinocoast.com).

GOLD RUSH DAYS

The discovery of gold on the South Fork American River in 1848 changed California from a remote farming outpost to a magnetic national destination. By 1850, the golden Sierra Nevada foothills had 100,000 new residents, all with big dreams of cashing in on the mother-lode. Despite the fact that the Gold Rush predated the Civil War and came and went within a decade, many lavish houses and Rush-era mining camps still thrive today.

Among potential highlights of a weekend in this area are white-water rafting on the American River, a night in a Victorian B&B, a leisurely autumn drive through Apple Hill's orchards, and a Hangtown Fry—an oyster and bacon omelet supposedly invented when a lucky prospector demanded the most expensive ingredients available—at Placerville's Hangtown Grill.

Contact: El Dorado County Chamber of Commerce (530-621-5885 or 800-457-6279; www.eldoradocounty.org).

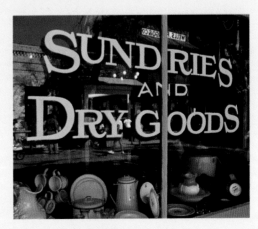

GENERAL STORE, COLUMBIA, CALIFORNIA

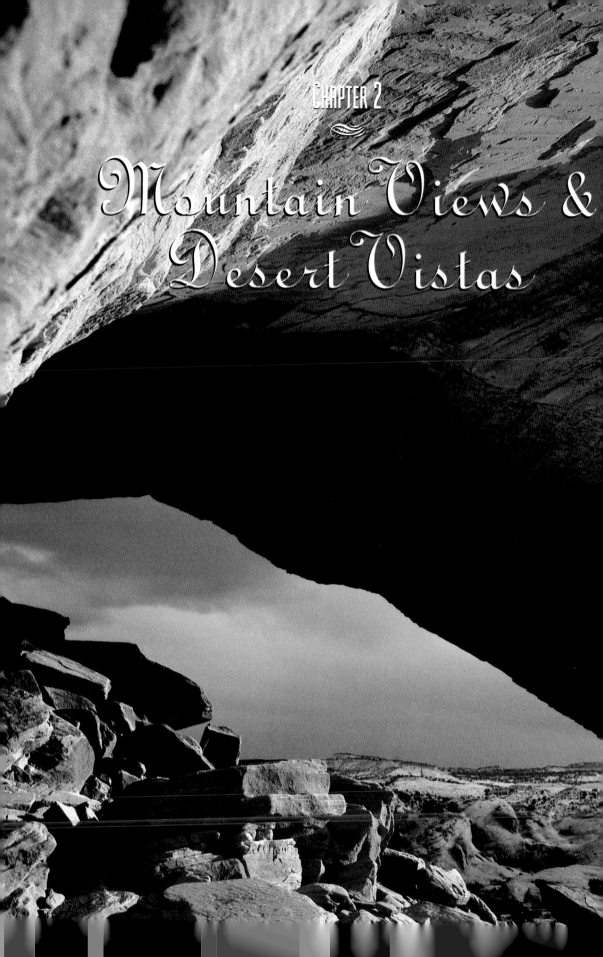

Chapter 2

Mountain Views & Desert Vistas

Southern Utah's Phipps Arch attests to the power of erosion to sculpt the land. Such amazing formations are common in the rugged canyon country of the Grand Staircase–Escalante National Monument.

THE WEST

Covering almost the entire mountain time zone, this tremendous region of the American West, north to south, is larger than all of Mexico. Almost everywhere you go here, you get a sense of limitless space. Hence weekend journeys, though plentiful, are scattered far and wide. But with careful planning, a traveler can zoom in on a spectacular place and come away a few days later refreshed and enriched.

The Four Corners states—Arizona, New Mexico, Colorado, and Utah—are characterized by their river-incised canyons and their ancient Native American history. The Rio Grande and the Colorado have been shaping this land for millennia, carving fantastic rock formations amid the high desert. Dinosaurs roamed the region long ago, leaving tracks and bones still visible in Utah. Long after those beasts died out, the Anasazi and their descendants, the Pueblo, came and built dwellings in the cliffs of Arizona and New Mexico.

The rivers left their timeless marks in places that have become national treasures, such as the Grand Canyon. We journey to the lesser known North Rim and the wild Arizona countryside above. Just north, the newly designated Grand Staircase-Escalante National Monument matches Connecticut in size. Over in Colorado, we take a look at the starker but equally dramatic Black Canyon of the Gunnison. And by looping through the mountains just west of Denver, you can walk some of the highest and most breathtaking peaks in all the Rockies.

Up in the open ranges of Wyoming and Montana, we travel through Big Sky country, where mining towns are pinpricks in a glorious landscape of vast cattle ranches backdropped by snow-crowned peaks. And for something entirely different, we journey to America's capital of glitz, Las Vegas, for a night or two of neon fun.

Glitter City

A uniquely American destination, Las Vegas first gained notoriety in the 1920s.

LAS VEGAS

Spring and fall are the most pleasant seasons in Las Vegas. Summer is blazing hot; winter nights can be freezing. Contact the Las Vegas Convention & Visitors Authority (3150 S. Paradise Rd., Las Vegas, NV 89109; 702-892-7575; www.vegasfreedom.com).

This desert outpost of gambling and neon lights was run by East Coast mobsters and ruled by Frank Sinatra's swingin' Rat Pack. In the 1990s, though, themed mega-resorts remade Sin City into a family-friendly, Disneyesque entertainment complex. Recently Las Vegas has reinvented itself again, building resorts that simulate European scenes and sophistication. A weekend in nouveau Vegas still leaves time for ferreting out what's left of the bad old days.

Though in the harsh light of day Las Vegas can look as homely as a show-girl without makeup, at dusk the city burns a gazillion kilowatts of lights. That's the time to hit the Strip: Las Vegas Boulevard. Here at Paris Las Vegas, a half-scale Eiffel Tower, a glass elevator rises 46 floors to a breathtaking observation deck.

More "Oh, wow!" architecture awaits at New York–New York, whose pop-art cityscape includes a facsimile of the Empire State Building and a 150-foot-tall Statue of Liberty. The casino's interior is themed as Central Park, complete with autumn foliage and a pond; the cashiers' cages are in the Financial District; the Greenwich Village food court features brownstone buildings and steam-emitting manhole covers. Swooping around (and through) the hotel, the hair-raising Manhattan Express roller coaster simulates the barrel roll of a jet fighter.

Farther up the street rises a black pyramid guarded by a ten-story-tall Sphinx. The Luxor, a 4,000-room hotel, has sides sheathed in some 27,000 plates of

Bright lights of Las Vegas attract shoppers, gamblers, and revelers to an assortment of around-the-clock entertainment, including shows by longtime local crooner Wayne Newton.

smoked glass. The xenon light projected from the apex of the pyramid is reputed to be the most powerful beam on Earth, equal to 40 billion candles. Nearby, the Venetian features a Doge's Palace, a Grand Canal where gondolas glide, and a museum of Impressionist and early modernist art. The Strip is also famous for its big shows, from the edgy performance art of Blue Man Group and Cirque de Soleil to the huge feathered headdresses of the long-running Folies Bergères. Magicians, crooners, dancers, and more perform year-round with seemingly endless energy.

Traces of Las Vegas's notorious past still thrive downtown, where the city began. A 1905 land auction near Main and Fremont Streets launched what everyone hoped would be a railroad boomtown. Saloons and a red-light district duly appeared. The city's oldest hotel, the 1906 Golden Gate, still stands on this corner, alongside pawn shops, adult motels, and instant-marriage chapels, like the Say I Do Wedding Drive-Thru.

Casino gambling was legalized in 1931, and the town's around-the-clock action lured vice-versed visitors. The first few

Dudes big and small get a feel for the saddle on a ranch near Escalante, Utah. In the days of the wild West, outlaws found hiding places among the area's labyrinthine canyons.

PREVIOUS PAGES: *Las Vegas's famous Luxor Hotel claims its light beams are visible from space. Inside are replicas of King Tut's tomb, sarcophagus, and other treasures, all handmade in Egypt.*

blocks of Fremont became Glitter Gulch, named for the flashing neon signs outside the gambling halls.

When tourists moved to the burgeoning Strip, downtown fell on hard times. To revive its appeal, in 1995 the city created the Fremont Street Experience, a four-block-long canopy lit up by 2.1 million lights and equipped with 540,000 loudspeaker watts to produce unforgettable sound-and-light shows.

Now bug-eyed tropical amphibians leapfrog entire blocks and space stations whirl against a background of stars.

Downtown offers visitors the chance to see Las Vegas as it used to be—a place for adults to misbehave. Before it became "gaming," gambling was raucous. Binion's Horseshoe gives a whiff of those days with its whorehouse decor and $15,000-a-hand maximum bet—still the highest stakes in town.

To Climb Up

From a Boulder Mountain overlook, as far as the eye can see—at least a hundred miles—stretch white cliffs and banded mesas. Set aside in September 1996, the Grand Staircase–Escalante National Monument encompasses 1.7 million acres of sandstone canyons, gullied plateaus, and weird rock formations in the high desert of southern Utah. Here you can lose yourself in the presence of boundless blue skies, intense sunlight, and silence broken only by faint breezes.

The size of this space is hard to grasp, even when you are staring in awe from Utah's Highway 12 on Boulder Mountain, nearly 9,500 feet up. A vast wilderness sur-rounded by yet more wild country, the monument extends from the Glen Canyon National Recreation Area and the Arizona border to Bryce Canyon National Park and Dixie National Forest. After Death Valley and Yellowstone, it is the largest park or monument in the contiguous United States.

The monument's name derives from two major geologic features: a series of sandstone plateaus stepping up more than 5,000 feet from the Colorado River to Bryce Canyon, and the Escalante River, which flows into the Colorado. One of the last rivers in the United States to be explored, the Escalante was named for Friar Silvestre Velez de Escalante, who passed through the area in 1776 after failing to find a route from Santa Fe to California's Spanish missions. Coincidentally, his name derives from a Spanish word meaning "to climb up."

This rugged and unforgiving terrain was crossed by a cavalry detachment in 1866, then rediscovered in 1872 by an exploratory team sent out by John Wesley Powell. Team geologist Clarence Dutton wrote a description that still holds: "It is a maze of cliffs and terraces lined off with stratification, of crumbling buttes, red and white domes, rock platforms gashed with profound cañons, burning plains barren even of sage—all glowing with color and flooded with blazing sunlight."

Actually, Dutton was not altogether accurate, or perhaps 125 years have altered the landscape. In fact, there is sagebrush—lots of it—as well as gnarled junipers, piñons, cactus, delicate wildflowers, and many other desert plants.

Today's explorers have a road to get them started. Snaking along the north edge of the monument, Utah 12 has been called one of the most scenic byways in America. From Escalante to Boulder, it weaves along red-rock cliffs and through slickrock canyons, at times following a knife-sharp ridge with sheer drop-offs and spectacular views on either side. The section of the road that crosses the

GRAND STAIRCASE

Escalante's spring and fall are the most moderate seasons. Summer temperatures can top 100°F, though the nights often cool to 60°F or below. Late summer brings frequent thunderstorms. Winter snowfall is light. Contact the Escalante Interagency Office (755 W. Main St., Escalante, UT 84726; 435-826-5499; www.utahcanyons.com). Always travel with food, water, a full tank of gas, and emergency supplies.

In formal regalia, Southern Paiute Indians pose on the rocky Kaibab Plateau in northern Arizona.
This 1873 photo captures a transitional time, when Paiute reservations were being established.

PREVIOUS PAGES: *Geologic art: An Escalante State Park hiker takes a breather, cradled in an intersection of grand stripes laid down in a canyon millions of years in the making.*

forbidding Aquarius Plateau was not completed until 1940 and paved in 1971. A more recently completed stretch runs from Boulder up to Torrey, through pine and aspen forests on Boulder Mountain, an area particularly gorgeous in autumn when the aspens turn gold and shimmer in the wind.

Small side roads, mostly dirt and gravel, peter out into foot trails that eventually give out, leaving an explorer in a potentially dangerous area. Names such as Carcass Canyon and Little Death Hollow are reminders that nature is still sovereign here. Some roads are impassable when wet. Flash floods in summer can make instant rivers out of dry washes and arroyos, or water-carved gullies.

With a weather eye out, then, you still should not miss a dip into the backcountry. A wonderful experience missed by most visitors, the Burr Trail Road heads southeast from the town of Boulder. If it were designated a scenic drive in a national park, the road would bear a steady stream of traffic, but only a small sign marks its entrance. The first 30 miles are paved, the road twisting through a canyon so narrow that the sky is just a wedge of blue way up between the walls.

Then the landscape becomes a giant's palace with huge pillars, temple gates, and archways. One good hike off this road, the Deer Creek Trail, becomes a scramble around rock tunnels and side canyons within a mile or so. You cross cascading pools and skirt high rock slopes that scratch the sky.

No Man's Land

Miles and miles of trackless desert and rangeland, unencumbered by civilization, roll ever onward to the plateaus and peaks of the far horizons. A few dirt roads cross the vast acreage, as noteworthy as stray threads on a carpet. The land is what matters here. Welcome to the Arizona Strip, an American outback, the no-man's land between the Grand Canyon and Utah. Harboring more than 8,000 square miles, the northwest corner of Arizona is home to a few thousand souls, nearly all of whom live in Fredonia or Colorado City. The rest of the land lies open like a lonely frontier, with one scenic highway nipping along the eastern portion through a luminist landscape of cliffs and buttes, meadows and forested plateaus.

As far back as 10,000 B.C., people came here to hunt and gather. Ancestral Pueblo

NORTHERN ARIZONA

In northern Arizona the weather varies depending upon location, season, and time of day. On the high plateau, expect a heavy winter, late spring, and pleasant summer. The lower desert areas can rise above 100° F on summer days. Contact Kaibab National Forest (430 S. Main St., Fredonia, AZ 86022; 928-643-7395; www.fs.fed.us/r3/kai/) or Grand Canyon National Park (National Geographic Visitor Center, Hwy. 64, Tusayan, AZ 86023; 928-638-2468; www.explorethecanyon.com).

people appeared around the time of Christ and raised corn, beans, and squash to supplement their diet of wild plants and game. Spanish Friars Dominguez and Escalante led the first Europeans into the area, arriving in 1776. A persistent problem for their ten-man team was food and water. On at least one occasion they had to eat a horse; locals gave them pine nuts, grass seeds, and cactus fruit. After their expedition, little changed in the area for a hundred years.

Then the Mormons began extending their reach from Utah to remote corners of the desert; they grazed their stock and set up tiny communities in the Arizona Strip. In 1893 the Grand Canyon Forest Reserve was established within its south and east portions, which became the Kaibab National Forest and the Grand Canyon National Park.

As whites began to settle the area, they encountered the relatives of the Kaibab Paiute, who live today on the remote Kaibab Indian Reservation. Within the reservation, the stamp-size Pipe Spring National Monument preserves a water source valued by Native Americans and pioneers in the 1800s. Though early travelers appreciated the beauty of this little oasis, modern eyes look outward and see a vast plain, cloud shadows floating atop baked mesas, buzzards drifting in a steel blue sky, and the Kaibab Plateau, 50 miles away.

Beyond this view lies an early traveler's nightmare: the Grand Canyon. Today the canyon is just two hours away in the air-conditioned comfort of a car. Along the way, the colors of the Arizona Strip reveal themselves—the purples and reds of the cliffs, the greens and yellow-browns of

the scrub desert, the oranges and pinks and whites of the rocks, and the blues of the distant mountains. In the waning days of fall, the sun casts long shadows of the Kaibab Plateau out across the desert. Up in the cool forest of the plateau, quaking aspens flame bright yellow against green ponderosa pines. In winter, snow up to eight feet thick blankets the high country.

The Kaibab Plateau is the highest of the five plateaus that make up the North Rim of the Grand Canyon. It tops 9,000 feet and collects a lot more wind and moisture than the lower areas of the Strip. A winding road ascends the plateau to the North Rim with majestic views along the way.

While no longer a secret, the North Rim attracts only eight percent of all Grand Canyon visitors. Visitors here are generally serious about the outdoors; they intend to get out and hike around and into the canyon. Views from this side are a little different: The canyon walls are higher and more dramatic. Even a short stroll out from Grand Canyon Lodge to Bright Angel Point gives one a dizzying feel for the canyon's amazing depth and width.

Diamond in the Rough

The jewel of the Sonoita Valley sits among oak grasslands at 4,050 feet, between southeastern Arizona's Santa Rita Mountains and the ochre-hued Patagonias, enjoying a reputation as a Western-flavored rural hamlet with an upscale Bohemian flair. A peaceful village of a thousand, many of them artisans, craftspeople, ranchers, naturalists, or retirees, Patagonia is situated

Grandiose interplays between sky and land await visitors to Patagonia's Circle Z Ranch, which since 1926 has offered riding and other activities on 6,500 acres at an elevation of 4,000 feet. Below, trail horses wait patiently as riders drink in the view.

beside two year-round creeks, making it one of the verdant oases in this semiarid high desert zone. Vineyards and apple orchards stitch green pinstripes across lion-yellow landscapes.

Day-trippers come to Patagonia for galleries and shops, restaurants and cafés. Old West history buffs roam back roads in search of ghost towns. Hiking and mountain biking enthusiasts use the town as a jumping-off place to trek the region's network of trails. Savvy sojourners favor the guest ranches tucked away in nearby hills and valleys. And birders travel from afar to study the region's bird-roosting areas, where hundreds of exotic species—and a good many travelers—find refuge.

Patagonia is a relative youngster, established in 1898 alongside the New Mexico & Arizona Railroad. Citizens voted to name it after the region in southern South America whose mountains and mines resembled those surrounding the town. Patagonia prospered as a shipping point for ore and livestock. Hotels and boardinghouses sprang up, followed by an opera house, restaurants, and saloons.

The mines petered out in 1959, and soon the railroad was out of business, too. But Patagonians turned the station grounds into a park and the abandoned depot into a town hall. Many vintage mercantile buildings are now residences; some have become artists' studios, too, open to interested patrons.

Sonoita and Harshaw Creeks splash through the central district, where streets are lined with large shade trees. About a mile from downtown, the Patagonia–Sonoita Creek Preserve is a veritable Eden amid a dun-colored landscape. Fluttery stands of willow and Fremont cottonwood create ideal perching and nesting places for hawks and herons. More than 160 species of birds, including the rose-throated becard, chatter above such earthbound neighbors as javelina pigs and desert tortoises.

Rocky Mountain High

In the upper Arkansas River Valley, the crags of the Sawatch Range etch the loftiest skyline in the Rockies. A 300-mile-long loop west of Denver takes in the peaks. There is nothing quite as exhilarating as walking on one of those mountainsides at 14,000 feet or more above sea level—unless it's the utter relaxation and bliss of soaking in a nearby thermal spring afterwards.

Some 12 miles south of Fremont Pass, 11,318 feet high, lies Leadville, a classic late-19th-century mining town. Situated at a lung-searing elevation of over

PATAGONIA

Patagonia is a year-round destination. Winters are mild, with occasional rain and light snow. Visit the information center in Patagonia (317 McKeown Ave., 520-394-0060 or 888-794-0060; www.patagoniaaz.com).

Into thin air: Situated at an elevation of more than 10,000 feet, the mining town of Leadville nestles in the shadow of the snow-blanketed Rockies, which rise several thousand feet above.

10,000 feet, the town is closer to heaven than any other incorporated community in the United States. Mounts Elbert and Massive tower above town to the west, while the Mosquito Range looms to the east. Wild West–type characters roam the sidewalk, and century-old red-brick buildings and rustic, false-fronted frame structures line the streets of downtown. Dedicated to the lore of ore,

the National Mining Hall of Fame & Museum includes a room filled with colorful, sparkling, indigenous crystals.

At 14,433 feet, Mount Elbert is Colorado's highest peak. Paradoxically, though, it is one of the "fourteeners": mountains in this area considered easier to summit because climbers begin their treks at such a relatively high elevation. The North Elbert Trail begins above

Rafters take on the frothy Arkansas River near Buena Vista, Colorado; afterward, they can refresh
and relax with a soak in one of the area's famous hot springs.
Opposite, in nearby Salida, another Arkansas River town, the Sculpture Park gives visitors
an entirely different sort of landscape to ponder.

10,000 feet and gains the summit after a steep 4.5-mile ascent. The longer, less strenuous South Elbert Trail starts at around 9,600 feet. Anyone considering either of these hikes should be wary of the symptoms of altitude sickness and, if they appear, should return to a lower elevation at once.

To the south, the colorful town of Buena Vista marks the turn-off for Cottonwood Hot Springs and Spa. The place has a decidedly New Age/old hippie ambience, with a lodge, rustic cabins, and tepees. Boulders set in concrete form cabinside pools in the shade of beefy cottonwood trees. Nearby, Mount Princeton Hot Springs Resort is just as enchanting. The afternoon light sparkles like liquid sunshine off the bubbling waters of Chalk Creek, a perennial source of purportedly healing waters.

Near Monarch Pass and the Continental Divide, at an elevation of 11,312 feet, the Monarch Crest Scenic Tramway offers an easy view from on high. The tram rises to an observation deck perched 700 vertical feet above the pass. You can enjoy close-up looks at gardens of tiny alpine wildflowers and near and far views of big, bare peaks reaching high above timberline, including Pike's Peak, some 70 miles northeast.

Not far east lies the attractive community of Salida, where new and old blend well. One of the town's bed-and-breakfast retreats, the Tudor Rose sits on a piñon-studded tableland nestled above town. The inn's 37 acres abut federal lands, providing access for hiking, mountain biking, and horseback riding on the heralded hundred-mile-long Rainbow Trail. Soak after a long day's hike at the popular and newly renovated Salida Hot Springs Aquatic Center, whose warm lap pool and hot sitting pools are filled with water heated by nature underground and pumped from nearby mountains.

Big Sky & Ghost Mines

Southwestern Montana's spacious landscape is replete with history, wildlife, big skies, trout rivers, and breathtaking mountain ranges. Ranching remains a primary industry, but mining was the business that inspired settlement here. Gold started things off, silver played a role, and finally copper made the biggest impact. Some early settlements became ghost towns; others still thrive.

An August morning in the Big Hole Valley: Mist rises from the river, flows across fields of freshly cut hay, and partially obscures the Bitterroot Mountains. High snowfields ignite with the warm light of dawn. The air is filled with the fragrance of growing things. The sky is a perfect blue, and no creature, no person seems to be in a hurry. It is

---

COLORADO ROCKIES

A year-round destination, the Colorado Rockies' higher trails are often snowed in until late June. Contact the Leadville Chamber of Commerce (809 Harrison Ave., P.O. Box 861, Leadville, CO 80461; 719-486-3900; www.leadvilleusa.com), or the Heart of the Rockies Chamber of Commerce (406 W. Hwy. 50, Salida, CO 81201; 719-539-2068 or 877-772-5432; www.salidachamber.org).

Sunlight pierces a dark sky over the Bitterroot Range of the Rocky Mountains. Running along the Idaho-Montana border, the range ranks among the most remote spots in the contiguous 48 states.

summer, a time of abundance—but the trouble is, summer has no lasting power. Fall comes early, winter is long, spring is uncertain. People here joke, "Summer? I missed it. I slept late that day."

In truth, a Montana summer can stretch out six weeks long or more. Everything feels right, from the meadowlarks on fence posts to the purple lupines bursting across alpine meadows. Even the scale is right. Numerous small ranges—the Tobacco Roots, Pintlers, Pioneers, and others—alternate with sage-covered foothills and green hayfields. The mountains have timber, the ranches have cows, the rivers have trout, and things seem to have been that way for a very long time.

The region has always been good for grazing, and it was well known to the Nez Perce Indians, who arrived here in 1877 from Idaho. Having crossed the Bitterroot Mountains, the Nez Perce paused to rest, thinking that they had left their pursuers—a detachment of the U.S. Army—behind. But a surprise attack had been planned, and, all told, 90 Nez Perce men, women, and children were slaughtered. Big Hole National Battlefield's sad but beautiful grounds help a visitor understand why those who have lived here love this region so passionately.

Mining brought white settlers into these lands and throughout the Rockies. Southwest Montana is a good place to track its development. In the beginning, prospectors wandered the countryside, panning for gold. Where they found

With a wooden sidewalk and a white picket fence, Victorian-era house in Virginia City, Montana, recalls the rich old days that followed the discovery of gold in nearby Alder Gulch in the early 1860s.

some, other prospectors would pour in. A tent village would pop up and become a beehive of activity, with men digging and sluicing and sometimes (if Hollywood has it right) yelling "Eureka!"

If the gold proved abundant, someone would seize the opportunity and build a sawmill. Soon wooden structures—shops, saloons, boardinghouses—stood, creating the start of a main street. Wagon roads and railroads got built to carry freight. Growing communities needed laborers and lawyers, tailors and teachers.

Many gold discoveries played out fast. Hopeful towns withered. The exceptions occurred where deep ore deposits justified underground mining. Then large companies took over, hiring hundreds of men and building mills, railroads, and smelters. Deep mines sometimes lasted long enough for a town to become permanent. Brick buildings and stone churches reflected plans for a stable future. When the mines failed, the men and women who served them might stay on and build a more lasting society, or they might move on.

Montana's first major gold strike occurred in 1862 at Bannack. Eventually, though, people moved on. Bannack is now a ghost town and state park. More than 50 buildings survive; most of them stand empty but speak volumes. The risks faced and the price paid by miners is evident today in the graveyard, whose stones record many early deaths.

Bannack was quickly overshadowed as Montana's predominant mining prospect by the fabulous strike at Alder Gulch. Virginia City grew up there and became notorious for the crooked sheriff Henry Plummer and the citizen-protectors who ended his outlaw activities. Plummer managed to become sheriff of both Virginia City and Bannack. Using his position to criminal advantage, he ran a gang of road agents called the Innocents, until the Montana Vigilantes lynched him in Bannack and put an end to his antics.

From Virginia City, the boom moved on, but this town did not die. Its history has been so well preserved, past and present can be difficult to separate. The lower end of Main Street is lined with one of the West's most complete collections of original wooden structures, hastily erected in the 1860s.

After Virginia City, Butte exploded. Called the "richest hill on earth," from the 1870s on it yielded more than 20 billion pounds of copper, clawed from thousands of miles of tunnels and shafts and, most visibly, the enormous Berkeley Pit. A hard, two-fisted town, Butte is still recovering from the closure of its vast mines in the 1980s. A visit here can tell powerful stories of immigrants staking out the land, of mine disasters and labor unrest, fortunes won and hardships endured.

Southwest Montana

Summer is the best time to visit Big Sky country; good fall weather can extend into October. Contact the Gold West Country Tourism Office (1155 Main St., Deer Lodge, MT 59722; 406-846-1943), which offers the "Southwest Montana Travel Guide."

MORE PANORAMAS

PUEBLO COUNTRY

As you drive the Ancient Way or walk the dusty roads of Acoma and other pueblos, you notice a stillness as big as the land itself. Looking out across ancient lava flows, you can see the Continental Divide and the Zuni Mountains, where ragged clouds gather like smoke signals, taking on the pink hue of the valley floor. Ravens glide like black arrows against the unbelievably blue sky. The air is thin, the sun intense, the sky very close.

The pueblo country south of I-40 between Albuquerque and the Arizona border may not startle you with its beauty. The high desert and its scattered mesas offer subtly changing tones and shadows, while the brown-and-white adobe buildings of centuries-old Indian villages cut neat patterns against the blue sky.

Contact: Albuquerque Convention & Visitors Bureau (505-842-9918 or 800-733-9918; www.itsatrip.org).

ADOBE WALLS OF TAOS, NEW MEXICO

TAOS

A 400-year-old Spanish colonial outpost in New Mexico's Sangre de Cristo Mountains, Taos exudes a remarkable peacefulness even at the peak of its summer tourist invasion. To many, Taos is simply quaint, chockablock with shops, galleries, museums, and antique adobes. To others, it is an exotic foray into American antiquity, with its feast days and festivals held in the shadow of Taos Mountain. Those who know Taos best, though, cherish its enduring qualities: the dramatic skies and crisp air, a strong sunlight capable of boosting colors to a wonderful intensity, and a sense of place engendered by its surrounding peaks.

Contact: Greater Taos Area Reservation and Information Network (505-758-3873 or 800-732-8267; www.taoschamber.com).

JURASSIC JOURNEYS

For 150 million years, beginning in the Triassic and continuing through the Jurassic and Cretaceous periods, dinosaurs roamed the land. Their day came to a sudden end some 65 million years ago, probably after a giant asteroid crashed into the Earth. Their times are chronicled in the fossil record they left behind, including in the high painted deserts of northeastern Utah. Begin your dinosaur tour at the North American Museum of Ancient Life, then stroll the dinosaur trackway at Red Fleet State Park in Vernal and witness

MISSION OF THE PUEBLO OF LAGUNA

hundreds of exposed fossil bones at Dinosaur National Monument.

Contact: Dinosaurland Travel Board (435-789-6932 or 800-477-5558; www.dinoland.com).

BLACK CANYON OF THE GUNNISON

Standing at the rim of the Black Canyon, you can see more than 2,000 feet down to the frothy green Gunnison River. Fins and spires of cold, dark rock plummet from a plateau of stunted trees to a netherworld of shadowy plinths and parapets. While the Colorado River was nudging through soft shale and sandstone to create the multicolored Grand Canyon, the Gunnison was chiseling into a different sort of rock: hard schist and gneiss. The result is a canyon that has not yielded easily to time. In this deep gash in the earth, shadows are the rule, sunlight the exception. Raptors ride the updrafts, and time is frozen into walls of stone 1.5 billion years old.

Contact: Black Canyon of the Gunnison National Park (970-641-2337; www.nps.gov/blca).

WYNKOOP BREWING CO., DENVER

into the largest brewery in the world, dozens of younger Colorado brew spots are far more intimate. A weekend brewery crawl might highlight a quaff at the Wynkoop Brewing Company (Denver's first modern brew pub), a Coors Brewery tour, a frothy Guinness at the Fado Irish Pub, and, in nearby Boulder, a crisp Claymore Scotch Ale at Mountain Sun Pub & Brewery or a cool draft at the Redstone Meadery.

Contact: Denver Metro Convention & Visitors Bureau (303-892-1112 or 800-233-6837; www.denver.org).

SHERIDAN, WYOMING

From the finely preserved old buildings along Main Street to the historic ranches in the surrounding hills, Sheridan would be a museum of the West's most alluring era if it weren't so fully alive today. The alpine meadows of the Bighorn Mountains empty into wide, green valleys, where you'll find not just cattle drives and fly-fishing streams, but Mediterranean nouvelle cuisine and afternoon polo matches. This is also one of the country's finest hang-gliding areas. Experts routinely spend an entire afternoon aloft; novices can take lessons. Dude ranches and B&Bs give an overnight taste of local life.

Contact: City of Sheridan Convention and Visitors Bureau (888-596-6787; www.sheridanwyoming.org).

BLACK CANYON OF THE GUNNISON NATIONAL PARK

DENVER AREA BREWERIES

Colorado is a hotbed of hearty beers. Maybe it's the mountain water—or perhaps the Prussian emigrant Adolph Coors, who, after landing in Colorado in the early 1870s, opened his Golden Brewery. Whereas Coors's creation was destined to evolve

CHAPTER 3

The Old Frontier

East Texas's Big Thicket National Preserve protects 86,000 acres of cypress swamps, pinelands, and savannas that once covered more than 3,000,000 acres. Plants and animals flourish here.

THE CENTRAL SOUTH

⟡

$\mathcal{T}$he south-central region of the United States blends heartland cowboy culture with south-of-the-border exoticism for a multi-ethnic gumbo served up in landscapes varying from hot desert to river delta. The weekend escapes in this chapter are places where you can rub shoulders with frontier history, get a taste of authentic small-town life, or dance with abandon to the beat of a sultry climate.

We start out with a visit to one of America's liveliest and most exotic cities, San Antonio. From the storied Alamo to the lovely Paseo del Rio, Latin American culture is evident here—in fact, Hispanics make up more than half the city's population. Next we travel to an unsung part of the Lone Star State—East Texas, where the region's timber and oil industries contributed to the nation's early development. Then we move on to another great American city. Just as there is only one New York, one Chicago, one Charleston—there is only one New Orleans. Only one place can be the most cosmopolitan, provincial, urbane, small-town, sophisticated,

PREVIOUS PAGE: *Massive columns help support Oak Alley Plantation, a spectacular 1830s Greek Revival mansion on the Mississippi River between New Orleans and Baton Rouge.*

earthy, multicultural metropolis in North America, all at the same time.

Moving on into the heartland, we pause in Eureka Springs, Arkansas, a spa town that never gave up the ghost. Farther north, the Missouri wine country offers an unexpected bit of sophistication and rich scenery along the bluffs, hills, and broad valleys of the Missouri River. The area's German immigrant history expands on the region's multicultural theme. Over in the Flint Hills of Kansas, more prairie earth surprises await.

We conclude the chapter with a quick tour of other places too good to overlook. The Texas hill country spreads west of San Antonio, and the rocky rivers and wild-flower-filled hillsides here seem a world apart from the state's sprawling cities. Likewise, the grand plantation houses outside of New Orleans are peaceful counterpoints to the bustle inside the city. And small towns like Guthrie, Oklahoma, and Abilene, Kansas, add a dollop of historic non-urban life.

Tejano Spirit

Serenading mariachi bands, spicy south-of-the-border cuisine, sultry tempera-tures, the buzz of Spanish mingling with English—you don't have to look far to immerse yourself in the vibrant Spanish and Latino culture that is San Antonio's heritage. Beloved for its colorful festivals and lively, danceable music, Mexican markets and tart margaritas, this spirited city in the heart of Texas offers

visitors a chance to delve right into a fascinating cultural kaleidoscope and to experience a modern city rooted deep in the region's past.

The city dates back to a late 17th-century Indian village and successive Spanish missions established along the San Antonio River in the early 1700s. The first mission, San Antonio de Valero, built in 1718, served a different purpose in the next century under its better known name, the Alamo. On March 6, 1836, during Texas' fight for independ-ence from Mexico, 189 Texan volunteers died heroes after a 13-day siege by Gen. Santa Anna's Mexican Army, choosing to stay inside the Alamo's walls rather than surrender. Only the chapel and the long barracks remain from the original com-pound, much larger than today's, but the spirit of those defenders—Jim Bowie and Davy Crockett among them—emanates throughout this sacred place.

Other missions south of town offer a glimpse of what life was like before independence. Each was a combination church, educational center, and farm, where priests worked to convert the local Native Americans to Catholicism. These structures—Missions Concepción, San José, San Juan, and Espada—are now part of San Antonio Mission National Historical Park. To gain more insight into San Antonio's history, one should spend some time at the Institute of Texan Cultures. Exhibits recount the contribu-tions of the various ethnic groups that have influenced Texas history.

Absorbed into the mural, musicians entertain at Mi Tierra Café and Bakery, a popular San Antonio hangout open 24 hours a day.

In the evening, the place to visit is the city's justly celebrated River Walk (Paseo del Rio), a festive, colorful three-mile stretch of shops, restaurants, clubs, and hotels along a loop of the San Antonio River, 20 feet below street level. Palms, olive trees, and cottonwoods shade flower-bedecked, Mexican-style buildings, inviting a stroll or a margarita at one of the romantic sidewalk cafes. Mexican restaurants are here in abundance, and sooner or later you'll pop into some place like Rio Rio Cantina, a big, loud, crowded, fun spot, for enchiladas or burritos.

On a second day, you could start the morning at bustling Market Square, composed of structures restored from the 19th and 20th centuries, a courtyard promenade, and El Mercado—the largest Mexican market in the United States. Piñatas, woven blankets, colorful pottery, leather, jewelry, and produce overflow

SAN ANTONIO

San Antonio can be visited year-round, although summers can be very hot. Contact the San Antonio Convention & Visitors Bureau (317 Alamo Plaza, San Antonio, TX 78298; 210-207-6700 or 800-447-3372; www.sanantoniovisit.com).

With swirls of color, dancers in the Ballet Folklorico de San Antonio reflect and energize the city's Latino heritage; in the non-summer months, the troupe travels throughout the United States.

PREVIOUS PAGES: *Visitors and locals throng riverside tables and tour boats along San Antonio's River Walk, a three-mile parade of shops, eateries, and native landscaping.*

dozens of shops, while adjacent Farmers Market Plaza boasts even more stalls. There's always entertainment in the plaza: a Tejano band or graceful flamenco dancers, artists and photographers displaying their works for sale. Nearby stands the impressive Spanish Governor's Palace, Spain's military headquarters in colonial times, located on the Plaza de Armas, the military parade ground in times gone by.

At some point, you should definitely head over to one of the city's longtime favorite restaurants. Open 24 hours a day, Mi Tierra Café and Bakery guarantees the flavor of old San Antonio. This market institution attracts a diverse array of customers hungry for chorizo (spicy sausage), huevos rancheros (Mexican-style eggs), and enchiladas. Be sure to leave room for delectable Mexican baked goods from the *panaderia.*

The Big Thicket

In the April dawn stillness, a kingfisher's harsh rattle rings out across a river lined with bald cypress and tupelo. A bobcat, its night of hunting finished, pads silently beneath a flowering dogwood, while in a boggy area nearby, a carnivorous pitcher plant stands ready to make a meal of an unwary insect. A swamp rabbit hears the high scream of a red-shouldered hawk and crouches even lower in its hiding place amid a living palette of wildflowers.

This is Texas? Yes, indeed: a region in the east that includes the Piney Woods and the swamplands of Big Thicket, bordering Louisiana and stretching from Arkansas south nearly to the Gulf Coast. Unlike far West Texas, which in some years is lucky to get 10 inches of rain a year, East Texas receives upwards of 50, an abundance that helps create the state's most diverse ecosystem. In this lush region, four national forests encompass varied wilderness areas, an important national preserve, hiking trails, canoeing streams, parks, and museums.

Just as the Piney Woods region is not all pines—oak, hickory, magnolia, beech, and sycamore make up an important component of the forest—neither is it all woods. Among the cities and towns dotting the area, the most interesting may be Jefferson, to the north, only 20 miles from Louisiana and Arkansas. Jefferson was a thriving steamboat port on Big Cypress Creek in the mid-1800s, but it saw its fortunes decline about one hundred years ago. To our benefit, that reversal preserved many fine old buildings.

The 1850s Excelsior Hotel stands out among dozens of historic structures; across the street rests the opulent railcar of Gilded Age tycoon Jay Gould, who is said to have predicted the town's demise when citizens spurned his offer of a railroad line. Not far to the east, bald cypress trees border the waterways of Caddo Lake State Park, where wood ducks, songbirds, beavers, and an occasional alligator delight wildlife-watchers who walk the park's trails or canoe its backwaters.

The area of East Texas traditionally called the Big Thicket is well known to biologists as one of the country's most diverse natural landscapes. It even contains cypress swamps. Much of this once vast ecosystem has been lost to development, but representative samples are protected within Big Thicket National Preserve, north of Beaumont. An international biosphere reserve, Big Thicket includes among its flora a wide variety of wildflowers, including 17 species of orchid and 4 types of insect-eating plants.

The forest that delights naturalists in East Texas today is only a shadow of the wilderness that European settlers found. Timbering since then has built entire towns. Lufkin's Texas Forestry Museum dedicates itself to that heritage, showing logging and sawmill techniques, equipment, and vehicles from the days when most work was done by hand.

EAST TEXAS

East Texas is a year-round destination, but heat, humidity, and mosquitoes make outdoor activities less pleasant in summer. Contact the Texas Tourism Division (800-888-8839; www.traveltex.com).

The East Texas Oil Museum tells of the frenzied days in 1930 following the gush of oil at the Daisy Bradford No. 3 well in Rusk County. Speculators and rowdies flooded in shortly after.

Another resource has had a powerful effect on the region: When wildcatters struck oil in Rusk County on October 3, 1930, they could hardly have known they had discovered the most productive petroleum field found anywhere up to that point. Fortunes were made overnight, and boomtowns—lively, dirty, and dangerous—sprang up just as quickly. The East Texas Oil Museum in Kilgore, one of the state's best small museums, uses innovative exhibits and audiovisual displays to recall that rough-and-tumble era.

Not far south, the Caddoan Mounds State Historical Park protects the burial and ceremonial sites of a Caddo Indian town that inhabited these lands from about A.D. 800 to 1300. With the help of displays and artifacts in the park museum, as well as a bit of creativity, you can walk through the site of an ancient village and imagine the advanced culture of these Native Americans. Much about their lives, beliefs, and fate still remains a mystery, however, awaiting the discoveries of a new generation of archaeologists.

Once Over Easy

Colorful. Flamboyant. Unique. New Orleans conjures up a wide array of images and adjectives that capture its food, music, and famous revels, including Mardi Gras. But the place is also rich in lore. A weekend exploring the French Quarter and beyond, learning how the "Big Easy" got its laid-back reputation, will always be an essential part of any American traveler's must-see list.

Founded by the French in 1718 on swampy land along the Mississippi River, New Orleans today would still be largely underwater if not for the surrounding levees, engineered to control the perennial drift of the Mississippi Delta. The Moon Walk promenades atop a riverside levee on the south edge of the French Quarter. Arrayed around the levee are the skyscrapers of the Central Business District (CBD to locals), the Crescent City Connection Bridge, the suburb of Algiers across the river, and the Mississippi itself, busy with barges and ocean-going ships.

Covering 90 square blocks to the north, the French Quarter (Vieux Carré) is where New Orleans began. Despite the name of that old neighborhood, New Orleans was a Spanish possession until the late 18th century. Many buildings are of Spanish design, built in the 1700s after fires razed earlier French-built structures.

In Jackson Square, gruesome public executions were conducted in the city's rebellious early days. The equestrian statue in the center of the flower-bright square honors Gen. Andrew Jackson, hero of the 1815 Battle of New Orleans. Dominating the square's north side (across Chartres Street) is St. Louis Cathedral, the nation's oldest active cathedral, built in 1794. But the most eye-catching thing about the square today is

NEW ORLEANS

Fall through spring are best; expect throngs at Mardi Gras (February) and Jazz Fest (April-May.) Contact the New Orleans Convention & Visitors Bureau (2020 St. Charles Ave., New Orleans, LA 70130; 504-566-5003 or 800-672-6124; ww.neworleanscvb.com).

the lively presence of fortune-tellers, street artists, and mimes.

At the southeast corner of Jackson Square, the arcades of the French Market, built in the 19th century as an open-air shopping area, run along Decatur Street. Among the shops, galleries, and restaurants here, the most famous is Café du Monde, which every year serves untold thousands of beignets (doughnut-like pastries) and cups of café au lait (chicory coffee with milk). This city landmark, open 24 hours a day, is a great place for people watching or late-night noshing.

The French Quarter also holds a number of fine historic houses that offer a glimpse into early lifestyles. Those open to the public include the Hermann-Grima Historic House, a federal-style brick home dating from 1831; the 1857 Gallier House, home of a prominent city architect; and the elegant Beauregard-Keyes House, built in 1826 and representative of a style called Raised American Cottage. Broke and looking for a job, Confederate Gen. Pierre Beauregard lived in a room here after the Civil War.

Just north lies famous (or is it infamous?) Bourbon Street, home of tacky tourist traps, raucous jazz and blues bars, and a big helping of New Orleans fun. A saunter along one of the best known streets in the country is de rigueur. Street scenes are especially wild and racy during Mardi Gras. Finally, no first-timers should leave New Orleans without visiting the quarter's Preservation Hall, where devoted musicians play nightly in a bare-bones setting. This taste of New Orleans heritage is worth the wait in line.

The much beloved St. Charles Streetcar, itself a national historic landmark, trundles west through another site so designated, the city's famed Garden District. From the mid-19th century until today, this neighborhood of mansions and gardens south of St. Charles Avenue has been among the most fashionable areas of New Orleans. Here, wealthy English-speaking residents lived apart from the francophones of the Vieux Carré. Many of the district's great ante-bellum houses are open to the public; guided tours of the area are safer than solo peregrinations. The Garden District also has one of New Orleans' "cities of the dead." The city's low-lying geography long required aboveground burials in elaborate tombs. These cemeteries have appeared in books and films, such as *Easy Rider*. For guaranteed entry, it's wisest to visit these evocative places on a guided tour.

Old-Fashioned Ozarks

Driving along winding roads through the Arkansas Ozarks and marveling at such a steep, narrow valley, a traveler naturally might wonder, "Who decided to put a town here?" To learn of Eureka Springs' birth is to understand how this picturesque village full of Victorian houses came to be preserved—and how it became a lively, colorful haven for artists, mystics, and eccentrics of all persuasions.

In the mid-1800s, settlers in the remote Ozark Mountains heard Native Americans tell of medicine springs back up in the hills. Occasionally an intrepid traveler would visit and come away claiming to have found relief from an illness or

Elaborate mortuary architecture including multitiered wall vaults and ornate family crypts—
New Orleans's answers to a water table too high for underground burial—creates cities of the
dead. Celebrating life, below, Mardi Gras revelers catch beads thrown from passing floats.

"Taking the waters" of Eureka Springs, Arkansas, once meant bathing in mineral springs. Here, a fisherman finds his own kind of therapy at a nearby lake.

infirmity. Before long, a makeshift settlement had grown up around the springs, and in 1879 it became an official town.

As it happened, Eureka Springs appeared on the map during a rampant American fad for "taking the waters," inspired by a general belief in the healing power of natural mineral springs. This Arkansas hideaway quickly became a popular spa. Six trains a day brought eager bathers, and fancy hotels and bathhouses sprang up to accommodate them. Eureka Springs turned boomtown, boasting gas streetlights in 1894 and electric streetcars in 1898.

But what booms often busts, and so went Eureka Springs, as modern medicine cast doubt on the power of spring water to cure disease. The "city that water built" sank into obscurity—and while other towns were tearing down their old buildings in the name of progress, Eureka Springs' endured.

Through the years, this beautiful setting continued to attract people longing for a peaceful retreat, including painters, writers, and craftspeople. In the counter-cultural sixties, back-to-the-landers found Eureka Springs an open-minded spot to drop out of one life and start another. "You could dream here and make it happen," one such immigrant recalls.

The legacy of all this is today's Eureka Springs: a town where streets lined with restored 19th-century houses wind along tree-covered hillsides, where quaint limestone buildings downtown are home to art galleries, shops, and restaurants, and where you're likely to see almost anyone walking down the sidewalk, from straitlaced businesspeople to aging flower children to successful artists to out-there spiritualists—sometimes all the same person.

Missouri Rhineland

The green hills and rolling farmland along the lower Missouri River seem at first like a typical midwestern landscape—but the country west of St. Louis holds a savory surprise. Nearly a dozen wineries cluster within just a couple of hours' drive here, offering travelers a weekend escape as flavorful as it is scenic and historical. The vineyards, and several quaint riverside towns, are in part the legacy of German immigrants who moved to this area in the middle of the 19th century, bringing with them Old World traditions that still echo along the tall bluffs of the Missouri River.

The pretty town of Hermann ranks as the best known of all the so-called German communities along the river. It makes a fine starting point for a winery tour. The town's first settlers, arriving in 1836, were from Philadelphia. Fearing that their European heritage was being diluted in that eastern city, they aimed to preserve their way of life in a new colony on the American frontier. Hermann still has streets named Mozart, Goethe, and

EUREKA SPRINGS

Spring and fall are the best times to visit Eureka Springs. Contact the Eureka Springs Chamber of Commerce (137B W. Van Buren St., Eureka Springs, AR 72632; 479-253-8737; www.eurekasprings.chamber.com).

Gutenberg, and it maintains much of its Old World flavor in architecture, food, and, of course, wine.

Hermann's wineries rank among the town's major attractions, and the best known and most historic may be Stone Hill Winery. Among the country's largest wine producers in the late 19th century, Stone Hill, like other wineries, was shut down during Prohibition, its vaulted cellars used for growing mushrooms instead. Revived in 1965, it again offers award-winning wines, including a fine red Norton. The winery's Vintage Restaurant, set in a renovated carriage house, is among Hermann's finest dining spots. It's a fitting place to lift a glass and toast vintage Missouri.

Another stop in Hermann, the Hermannhof Winery, is housed in an imposing brick building downtown. As is the case at many wineries, Hermannhof sells locally made cheese, bread, and sausage for an impromptu picnic, perhaps along the Missouri riverbank just a short stroll away. Two miles southwest, the Adam Puchta Winery is the state's oldest winery still owned by the original family. The sixth generation

of Puchtas is producing wine in this quiet setting on the bank of Frene Creek.

The next day, those in need of exercise may want to head to Katy Trail State Park, a 225-mile hiking and biking route that follows the converted trailbed of the Missouri-Kansas-Texas Railroad (the "Katy line"). Small towns and inns along the way offer the chance for overnight trips. One could then spend a leisurely afternoon rambling along the Missouri east of Hermann, stopping in at New Haven's Röbller Vineyard, known for its Norton reds.

Scenic highways follow both the north and south banks of the Missouri River. Lying in the foothills of the Ozarks, the countryside is characterized by steep hills dotted with woodlands and high plateaus overlooking the river's fertile bottomlands. There's a humid, languorous quality to summers here, when cicadas rasp in the trees and a sultry haze veils the hills. To the west, the town of Augusta became America's first federally designated wine district in 1980, but wine was being produced well over a century ago at Mount Pleasant Vineyards. This sophisticated oasis sits on a breezy hilltop overlooking a broad floodplain, created when the Missouri River once shifted its course.

MISSOURI RHINELAND

Spring bloom through fall harvest are the best times for touring Missouri's vineyards. Contact the Hermann Welcome Center (312 Market St., Hermann, MO 65041; 573-486-2744 or 800-932-8687; www.hermannmo.com).

Prairie Earth

People who say that Kansas is flat have never visited the Flint Hills. They've never driven along a Chase County

Spirited oompah bands add brass to festivals, parades, and special events in Hermann, Missouri. Octoberfest and Maifest highlight the town's German heritage.

creek bottom bordered by rolling ridge-lines, never climbed to the top of one of those ridges and looked out over the crests and valleys stretching beyond the horizon, never heard the song of a meadowlark fluting across the grassland and cottonwoods. Those who have done those things will never think of the state as just flat cornfields again.

Extending in an irregular band north to south across Kansas nearly from border to border, the Flint Hills were named for the hard flint (or chert) rock interbedded with the predominant underlying lime-stone here. Settlers learned early on that most of this region was unsuitable for farming; the rocky ground resisted the plow, and crop production was poor. But the lush prairie grasses provided fine grazing for cattle, and today—except for scattered small towns and limited bottom-land agriculture—nearly all of the Flint Hills is devoted to ranching. History, nature (including a new national preserve), and a strong Western heritage converge in the central part of the area, offering travelers a journey into a diverse and intriguing landscape.

A sense of the past is ever present in Council Grove. Here an 1825 council meeting between U.S. government officials and Osage chiefs allowed passage

The Second Empire splendor of the 1873 Chase County Courthouse in Cottonwood Falls, Kansas's oldest courthouse still in use, adds dimension to flat prairie land all around.

across the Neosho River amid a grove of oaks and other hardwoods, through Indian lands, in exchange for $800. Soon the Santa Fe Trail passed through here on a path from today's Missouri to New Mexico, becoming one of 19th-century America's most important trade routes. A trading post developed at Council Grove, where trees provided shelter and wood for wagon repairs to travelers heading west from Independence, Missouri, to Santa Fe.

Eventually a thriving settlement grew up at this natural gathering place along the river, and many structures still endure from those pioneer times. The Hays House Restaurant serves home-style food in a building constructed in 1857 by Seth Hays, the founder of Council Grove. Over the years this building has been a post office, a court-house, and a church, and it now calls itself the oldest continuously operating restaurant west of the Mississippi. Just down the street, the 1851 stone building at Kaw Mission State Historic Site was a school for children of the Kaw, or Kansa, tribe, the Native Americans for whom Kansas was named.

Stretching for two miles along both sides of Highway 177, north of Strong City, the Tallgrass Prairie National Preserve was created in 1996 after many years of often bitter controversy. Conservationists wanted a national park dedicated to preserving a portion of the once vast tallgrass prairie, one of America's most endangered ecosystems; local ranchers fought against govern-ment acquisition of Flint Hills grazing land. As a compromise, most of the

preserve's 10,894 acres are owned by the private National Park Trust, although the land is managed by the National Park Service.

Dominating the scene in Cottonwood Falls, the 1873 Chase County Courthouse rises impressively on the town square, its mansard roof topped with an ornate cupola. As imposing as its native lime-stone exterior is, though, the courthouse's glory is its spiral staircase, made of black walnut cut from the banks of the Cottonwood River and rising three stories in graceful curves, one complete circle for each floor.

Outside town, back roads form the Sharpe's Creek Drive, a 20-mile route through some of the finest scenery in the Flint Hills. Beginning in the tiny hamlet of Bazaar, the drive heads south and then west, passing open rangeland where ridgetops offer ter-rific views of the prairie.

The Cassoday Café in the small town of Cassoday is a local favorite. Here you're likely to see cowboys—real ones—taking a break from herding cat-tle on nearby ranches. You have to like a place with a sign out front that reads, "Good Food and Gossip—Established 1879." ≈

FLINT HILLS

In the Flint Hills, winter can bring very cold temperatures and, rarely, blizzards. Contact the Kansas Travel and Tourism Development Division (700 S.W. Harrison St., Suite 1300, Topeka, KS 66603; 800-252-6727; www.travelks.com).

FURTHER STAKEOUTS

NOTTOWAY PLANTATION, WHITE CASTLE, LOUISIANA

TEXAS HILL COUNTRY

Generations of Texans have revered the place they call the Hill Country—known for wildflower meadows, oak-juniper woodlands, and clear, cool rivers. This rugged landscape northwest of San Antonio remains true to the spirit of the cowboys who've been jangling their spurs here for over a century, with enough ten-gallon hats, riding trails, and dude ranches to satisfy any traveler with a yearning for the Old West. The Hill Country was settled in part by Polish and German immigrants, and today its small towns offer a blend of Old World traditions and pure Texas cowboy heritage, adding up to a destination as full of delights as it is beautiful. Contact: Bandera Texas Convention & Visitors Bureau (830-796-3045 or 800-364-3833; www.banderacowboycapital.com).

Not to be missed are the ornate interiors at San Francisco Plantation in Garyville, and the spectacular Nottoway Plantation in White Castle, famous for its early indoor plumbing. The River Road African American Museum near Sorrento is also enlightening. And it would be a shame to pass up the Cajun-style seafood and white-chocolate bread pudding in Donaldsonville's Grapevine Market and Café. Contact: Ascension Parish Tourist Commission, 6967 Hwy 22, Sorrento, LA 70778 (225-675-6550 or 888-775-7990; www.ascensiontourism.com).

COWBOY HERDS CATTLE IN TEXAS HILLS

ROAMIN' OAKS

Antebellum planters built showplace mansions on the lower Mississippi, the watery Main Street linking their lands. Several surviving structures between Baton Rouge and New Orleans can be toured today. Some have been restored to glittering splendor. Others are more historic than elegant. All provide a peek inside a vanished era.

GUTHRIE

The streets of downtown Guthrie, Oklahoma—lined then as they are now with handsome redbrick and sandstone buildings—hummed in the late 1880s with commerce and political deal-making befitting the state's new capital. Nowadays, though it's no longer the Sooner State's major metropolis, this community just north of Oklahoma City stands proudly today as a veritable time capsule of early 20th-century architecture. Guthrie is also a lively town full of inns and shops in one of the Midwest's most historically significant settings.

One friendly local hangout, the Blue Belle Saloon, features a tile floor, tin ceiling, and superb wood back bar. If you'd dropped in here in 1902, you could have chatted with a bartender named Tom Mix, who later moved to Hollywood and became a famous cowboy-movie star during the silent era.

Contact: Guthrie Convention and Visitors Bureau (212 W. Oklahoma Ave., 405-282-1947 or 800-299-1889; www.guthrieok.com).

ANNUAL 89ER DAY PARADE, GUTHRIE, OKLAHOMA

ABILENE

Amid the wheat fields and rangeland of central Kansas sits one of the legendary towns of the Old West: Abilene, where lawman Wild Bill Hickok kept an eye out as rowdy cowboys spent their wages on whiskey and women. Nineteenth-century America had a number of famous cowtowns—places like Wichita, Dodge City, and Fort Worth. Some have changed to match the times, but Abilene still fits the original rawhide mold. These days the town is

a peaceful community, more in the spirit of the first city marshal, Tom Smith, who enforced a "no-guns" policy in the town.

Abilene, Kansas, also proudly claims Dwight D. Eisenhower, World War II general and one of America's most popular presidents, as a native son. His home and grave are here, part of the Dwight D. Eisenhower Library, a national repository containing presidential papers and artifacts from the war through his 1950s administration. Other lively arts and culture, theater, museums, and exhibits aplenty keep anyone visiting Abilene as happily busy as a cowboy celebrating the end of a cattle drive.

Contact: Abilene Convention & Visitors Bureau (785-263-2231 or 800-569-5915; www.abilene.com/visitors).

LEBOLD-VAHSHOLTZ HOUSE, ABILENE, KANSAS

Chapter 4

North Country Explorations

American bison graze prairie grass in North Dakota. Tens of millions of bison roamed the continent before European settlement; some 65,000 now live in parks and private rangelands.

THE MIDWEST

From the Great Plains to the Great Lakes, from midwestern prairie to middle-American town, this nation's north country takes in a mighty swath of territory. It was to these cold climes that German and Scandinavian immigrants made their way, turning wild prairies into productive farmlands and putting down roots that still remain. Others moved on: Pioneers heading west through the prairies sometimes felt as though they were sailing a sea of grass, noting in their diaries an occasional rocky cliff or outcropping as if they were sighting land. The Great Lakes and Plains may not be known for relief, but subtle beauties endure—the echo of a loon's call, early morning light on a frozen lake, summer wildflowers in tall grass.

To get a feel for the early days, we journey along Lewis and Clark's trail in North Dakota. Much has changed in the last 200 years, but long views remain, and fort sites and museums help you peer into the past. This region is also where the Father of Waters begins its long journey down the nation's midrift: In northern Minnesota you can actually step across the headwaters of the Mississippi River.

Those who say that this region has no vertical relief are forgetting the manmade. One of the great American cities, Chicago soars above Lake Michigan. We focus on its skyline, filled with treasures of 20th-century architecture, and glance at another, smaller city—Columbus, Indiana—also noted for graceful modern buildings.

Scattered all over the Great Plains and Great Lakes region are the small towns, attractive and friendly, on which this country prides itself. De Smet, South Dakota, and Galena, Illinois, are villages that have, like well-tended bonsai, aged well without growing big. The Amana Colonies in Iowa and the Amish community of Berlin, Ohio, have rich histories rooted in religion and agriculture; Michigan's Mackinac Island, Wisconsin's Ephraim, and Ohio's Lake Erie Islands have long histories as Great Lakes resorts.

Land of Lewis & Clark

Dominated by North Dakota's Lake Sakakawea recreational area, this region opens a window on the time when Native Americans grew crops around earth-lodge villages. Bison, grizzlies, wolves, and elk still roamed the prairie. European settlers were scarcely more than a rumor among the Plains Indians. On their journey 200 years ago, Meriwether Lewis and William Clark set up camp here.

Eventually, white settlers moved in. Dams were built. The Garrison Dam created Lake Sakakawea, submerging 178 miles of river channel. Yet despite the dramatically altered landscape, it is still possible to see country that looks much as it did when the explorers came through. At the lake's upstream end, badlands and wooded coulees give the impression of wilderness untamed. And while watercraft buzz up and down the reservoir, the shores remain wild, with only occasional clusters of summer cabins.

Below the lake, the river rolls through fertile bottomland thick with cotton-woods and wildlife. Cross Ranch State Park, which protects a 589-acre natural area, is a good place to begin a journey. White pelicans fly over the river; deer and coyotes shelter in the forest. At Washburn, the Lewis and Clark Interpretive Center offers evocative artwork, displays, and objects, including a 28-foot facsimile dugout canoe. The original canoe—smallest of the expedition—carried about 3,000 pounds.

The explorers carved their canoes during the winter of 1804-05, while living in a triangular log stockade near the river. Fort Mandan Historic Site, near the original location, offers a reproduction of that simple log shelter among the cottonwoods. Twenty-five years later, fur traders built another fort a few miles upstream. Called Fort Clark, it was made famous by Karl Bodmer, a Swiss artist who spent the winter of 1833-34 here. His paintings of the landscape and its people are as

On the trail of Lewis and Clark in 1833, artist Karl Bodmer (far right) and German naturalist Prince Maximilian meet with Minatarre, or Hidatsa, Indians at Fort Clark, North Dakota, in this aquatint etching.

detailed as photographs, showing winter camps, earth lodges, dogs pulling toboggans, and Mandan chiefs.

All that remains at today's Fort Clark State Historic Site are a barely visible fort foundation and 200-some circular depressions marking locations of Mandan earth lodges. The story is a sad one: In 1837 a steamboat brought smallpox, which nearly destroyed the community. Survivors moved north to a site now beneath the lake.

At Knife River Indian Villages National Historic Site, a museum and reconstructed earth lodge help fill in the picture. You can't help but admire the simple, efficient architecture. In the early 1800s, five villages stood here. Now only circular depressions remain. At one of these villages the explorers met the fur trader Toussaint Charbonneau, who with his

LEWIS & CLARK

Summer and fall are best for a visit to Lewis and Clark territory. Contact the North Dakota Tourism Department (604 E. Boulevard Ave., Bismarck, ND 58505; 701-328-2525 or 800-435-5663; www.ndtourism.com).

Nothing, not even the snows of winter, can stop the mighty Mississippi from rolling on.
At its traditional headwaters in Minnesota's Lake Itasca, the river runs clear and shallow.

Shoshone wife, Sacagawea, agreed to accompany the expedition. The lake nearby was named for her.

At the lake's eastern end, shoreline marshes of the Audubon National Wildlife Refuge were designated to replace wildlife habitat lost beneath the reservoir. The lake's central part is surrounded by Fort Berthold Indian Reservation, home of the Three Affiliated Tribes: Mandan, Arikara, and Hidatsa. Summer powwows, which feature traditional dancing and drumming, are high-spirited religious and social events where everyone is welcome.

A River is Born

Where a shallow stream flows out from a forest-rimmed lake in northern Minnesota, the Mississippi River begins its long journey. The headwaters region is a landscape of lakes, marshes, and forests, filled with wildlife and outdoor opportunities. It offers old-growth forest, hidden bogs, canoeing rivers, bicycle trails, lakeside cabins, Paul Bunyan legends, and a glimpse of logging history.

Minnesota is one-tenth water. But the landscape around Bemidji and Park Rapids looks wetter than that. Lakes are everywhere. Roads wind around their shores. Loons float on calm waters, their long, mournful calls the anthem of

MISSISSIPPI WATERS

The Mississippi headwaters area is best in late summer, though autumn colors and winter activities have their devotees. Contact Park Rapids Area Chamber of Commerce (P.O. Box 249, Park Rapids, MN 56470; 218-732-4111 or 800-247-0054; www.parkrapids.com).

Life-size Paul Bunyan gives children a helping hand in Akeley, Minnesota.

the north. Great blue herons wade in the marshes among dome-shaped houses built by beavers. Shallow bays are thick with wild rice, still harvested each fall by Ojibwa, who bend stalks over canoes and knock grains free with sticks.

In 1832 Indian agent Henry Schoolcraft was guided by Ozawindeb to the outlet of a narrow lake that he declared the true source of the Mississippi River. He coined the name Itasca from the Latin *veritas caput,* or "pure head." The Ojibwa called the lake Omushkos, Elk Lake. They knew it well and understood that the waters flowed downhill from this point.

The Indians felt no need to distinguish one stream as the official headwaters. So how was it decided that out of this particular area of the Mississippi's huge basin flowed the mighty river? The Ohio River has greater volume, the Missouri is longer and falls from a higher elevation, and yet the two rivers are considered tributaries. Several streams flow into Lake Itasca, but Henry Schoolcraft thought them too small to qualify as rivers. In the end, no hard rules apply. In this case, 150 years of tradition matter as much as anything else.

This region also gave rise to the legend of Paul Bunyan, said to have been born in Bemidji and to have grown as tall as the trees he cut. On his first birthday, his father gave him Babe, a blue ox, and together they changed the shape of the north. Never mind what geologists say: Popular legend tells us that the Mississippi River started when Paul and Babe's water-tank wagon sprang a leak. Area lakes are just Babe's hoofprints.

Paul Bunyan's trees were primarily red pine and eastern white pine—excellent lumber used in houses, barns, and churches throughout the Midwest and across the treeless plains. In the loggers' wake, there grew up a second-growth forest of aspen, maple, birch, oak, and other broadleaf species, different from the original but still a beautiful backdrop to family cabins and lakeshore resorts that started as fishing camps. Turn-of-the-20th-century vacationers hopped trains going north to rusticate in the woods.

Today resorts have gone modern, with flush toilets, microwaves, satellite dishes, and Internet connections. And while fishing is still important, visitors now also come for bicycling, canoeing, hiking, skiing, snowmobiling, or enjoying the forest in its seasonal glory. Spring is wildflower season: trillium, bloodroot, bellwort, showy lady's slipper. In summer, green piles upon green. In fall, the mixed hardwoods explode with color.

There's no better place for exploring than Itasca State Park. Established in 1891, the park protects the source of the Mississippi and preserves a tract of pre-Bunyan woodland. A shallow stream of clear water slides out from beneath wild rice at the lake's outlet to become the great Mississippi, America's central waterway. At this point, children hop easily across the river on stepping-stones, yet you can almost feel the connection with the great Gulf of Mexico, more than 1,400 feet lower and 2,350 river miles away.

Inspired Community

In an amphitheater of gentle hills carved by the Iowa River lies a ring of seven villages, built nearly 150 years ago by a group of German religious refugees. Their successful experiment in deliberate, peaceful living continues to this day amid the bucolic splendor of eastern Iowa. Visitors are welcome to stroll past sturdy cedar-sided houses and post-and-beam barns, to visit the workshops, wineries, museums, and restaurants of this Utopian enclave just a few miles off the interstate.

In 1855, when Buffalo, New York, grew too crowded for Christian Metz and his Community of True Inspiration, they moved west into the new state of Iowa.

Clothing from the 19th century hangs in the Museum of Amana History, which evokes a picture of the early life of the Christian utopian community, still active in eastern Iowa.

They had come from Germany 13 years earlier, seeking a place to live and worship in peace. They found what they were looking for in the Iowa River Valley, and in time the community of 1,200 souls bought a 26,000-acre parcel of farmland and began building.

The Inspirationists believed that they received the word of God not only through the Bible and in moments of quiet, but also through "instruments," or chosen people. Christian Metz was one; Barbara Heinemann, the last, died in 1883. Scribes followed these instruments around so that nothing would be missed when the spirit moved them. The recorded testimonies remain a key part of the community faith.

Each village was laid out along orderly Old World lines, with barns at one end, workshops at the other, and orchards and vineyards on the edge of town. A 16-mile loop connects the seven villages, which were spaced about an hour's ox-cart drive apart. The village of Amana was the first

AMANA COLONIES

Peak season in the Amanas runs from May through September. Contact the Amana Colonies Convention and Visitors Bureau (Visitor Center, 39 38th Ave., Ste. 100, Amana, IA 52203; 319-622-7622 or 800-579-2294; www.amanacolonies.com/visitor).

established, and it is now the site of the Museum of Amana History, housed in an 1864 home and an 1870 schoolhouse.

The Amana Colonies were a communal society, sharing housing, medical care, food, jobs, and education. But hard times hit the area, along with dissatisfaction within the community, and in 1932 the people voted to separate economically from the church, with members receiving shares of stock.

Many old-timers still vividly remember the Great Change. Although some "didn't think much of it," it enabled the community to adapt to modern life. The people of the Amana Colonies bought cars and started their own businesses. One enterprising villager started a company that grew into Amana Appliances, now a national manufacturer of refrigerators and air conditioners. Though people sometimes confuse the Amana community with the Amish, all the two share is their German heritage. In Amana, technology is fine—think refrigerators, not horsedrawn buggies.

Of all seven villages, Amana possesses the highest concentration of shops and restaurants and thus the most touristy feel. It's still a leisurely drive or walk along unhurried streets to visit shops that sell handcrafted furniture, sweet wines, smoked meats, and colorful woolens. At the Amana Woolen Mill, dating from 1857, you can walk through the weaving room, thumping with the sound of machine looms, and quickly realize that Amana is not stuck in the past. The oldest looms here are from the 1940s, but the newer ones can turn out a six-foot blanket in less than four minutes.

Trellises arch over lush gardens; children play behind old brick and sandstone houses. At the west end of town lies the calmest place of all, the village cemetery. Each village has its own little graveyard, with neat rows of small, uniform headstones, like a parallel and even more peaceful village of ancestors. In the 1960s, English-language church services were added to the traditional German, but despite such changes, much remains the same in the Amanas. "We're a little like *Fiddler on the Roof*," one villager says. "We use the word 'tradition' a lot."

Top-Floor Chicago

Along the shore of Lake Michigan, Chicago's towers of stone and steel explode from ground to sky, a dizzying spectacle. With its magnificent array of early and modern skyscrapers, this city is sometimes grandly referred to as Paris on the Prairie. Simply put, Chicago is a feast for the eyes, a vast open-air museum. But its architecture is not merely about size or looks: It is also about innovation. For here, early 20th-century architects—some of the world's master builders—dared to go higher than ever, using techniques never before tested.

The Great Chicago Fire of 1871 destroyed a third of the city's buildings. Soon a new Chicago began to rise. Architect Daniel Burnham's 1909 plan

Chicago's pumped-up skyline features the 110-story Sears Tower, tallest building in North America; its steel and concrete caissons are embedded in rock hundreds of feet below the ground.

All right angles and straight edges, Unity Temple in Chicago's Oak Park is a Frank Lloyd Wright masterwork of foursquare simplicity.

PREVIOUS PAGES: *In Chicago's Rookery, graceful staircase of marble catches light from abundant windows. Burnham & Root designed the building in 1888; Frank Lloyd Wright remodeled it in 1906.*

envisioned a monumental city of wide avenues and grand public parks and buildings. As a result, today's Chicago is a collection of 20th-century architectural landmarks, designed by the likes of Frank Lloyd Wright, Louis H. Sullivan, and Dankmar Adler. You'll find their hand-

CHICAGO

Chicago's biting winds blow off the frozen lake in winter; spring and fall are generally mild; summers can be hot and humid. Contact the Chicago Architecture Foundation (224 S. Michigan Ave., Chicago, IL 60604; 312-922-3432; www.architecture.org).

work clustered inside the Loop area, bounded by the El subway system.

One of the most famous buildings, the 1888 Rookery Building, was an important precursor to the skyscraper; it features a masonry base, terra-cotta ornamentation, and a stunning atrium designed by Frank Lloyd Wright. Revolutionary in its plain exterior, the 1889-91 Monadnock Building represents early skyscraper techniques, its 16 stories supported by six-foot-thick ground-floor walls built atop an iron raft. The 1891 Manhattan Building incorporates newer metal-frame construction techniques, unique bay windows, and an upper brick façade.

As the world's buildings grew taller, so did those in Chicago, the most famous of which is the 110-floor Sears Tower, North America's tallest skyscraper, built in 1973. A top-floor deck offers a breathtaking bird's-eye view, day and night. The observation deck of the John Hancock Center, one hundred stories tall, offers another spectacular 360-degree perspective. Visitors can relax in the restaurant-bar on the building's 94th floor and watch Lake Michigan darken as the city begins to sizzle with light.

A good plan for a second day in Chicago is to explore the leafy Oak Park neighborhood, about ten miles west of the Loop. Frank Lloyd Wright made his mark here between 1889 and 1909, developing his signature prairie style in 25 buildings and houses—the world's largest concentration of his work. At the Frank Lloyd Wright Home and Studio one can tour his residence and see how he emphasized large, open, free-flowing spaces. The house also contains Wright-designed furniture and decorative objects.

One Wright must-see, the Unity Temple—built to house a Unitarian Universalist congregation—has been in use since 1908. Dubbed "my little jewel box" by the architect, its unprecedented cubist design features abundant concrete and an unusual receding flow of interior space. The light and silence in this space are magical. Also in Oak Park, the Cheney House Bed & Breakfast was built by Wright in 1903 for a young couple; the wife later became Wright's lover. The B&B offers the chance to sleep in an authentic prairie-school house. Even the bedspreads were designed by Wright.

No Cars Allowed

It only takes 20 minutes, but the short, bracing ferry ride from Michigan's Lower Peninsula across the Straits of Mackinac (pronounced MACK-in-aw) carries you a century back in time. Mackinac Island has lured generations of vacationers with its well-preserved air of Victoriana, its outdoor enticements, and its beauty. Whether you stay a day or a month, you'll vow to come back to this enchanted isle of horse-drawn carriages, splendid cottages, and pine-scented trails.

On the approach to Mackinac across the waters of Lake Huron, you can see the island's humped back rising higher than others in the straits. For good reason, then, the Ojibwa called it Michilimackinac, "great turtle." The wooded bluffs, highlighted by the spanking white colonnade of the Grand Hotel, yield on the island's south corner to a throng of turreted Victorian buildings gaily crowding the harbor. Here you disembark into the bustle of liveried porters, bicycle bells, and keening gulls.

The first thing you notice on Mackinac Island is the absence of cars. No honks, no smells, no rush-hour traffic, but instead the clip-clop of horse hooves and the occasional whir of bicycles, echoing along

MACKINAC ISLAND

Summer is high season on Mackinac Island; fall's cooler days are also excellent for a visit. Contact the Mackinac Island Tourism Bureau (P.O. Box 451, Mackinac Island, MI 49757; 906-847-3783 or 800-454-5227; www.mackinacisland.org).

Old ways never die on Michigan's Mackinac Island, where horse-drawn carriages are the only way to travel other than by bicycle or foot. The geranium-adorned 660-foot-long front porch of Mackinac's Grand Hotel, opposite, provides relaxing views of Lake Michigan. The 1887 hotel offers such old-time delights as high tea, croquet, and chamber music.

A patient woman sews quilts in Berlin, Ohio, the world's largest Amish community.
Curious outsiders provide a steady market for these carefully handcrafted items.

shady lanes. Motor vehicles were banned in 1898, and today's islanders like it just fine. Boats and planes deliver groceries, mail, supplies, and tourists to the docks. Carriages take things from there.

Sooner or later everyone ends up on Main Street (officially, Huron Street), just off the ferry docks. In fact, many people get no farther than a stroll along Main, with its charming little shops and a dozen or so fudge confectionaries.

The smell of fudge is so pervasive that it's hard to resist stopping for a sample or two. Though no one appears to know exactly when it first appeared on Mackinac, fudge is a tradition dating back to the 1880s. Murdick's and Ryba's are two veterans in the trade, the latter having gone into high gear in the 1960s with fans to waft the odors into the street. Inside you can watch chocolate being poured from copper kettles onto cool marble slabs. Savor a bite of rum-black walnut or pistachio-pecan.

Behind Main, Market Street is a relatively quiet lane of lilacs, lampposts, and old houses with hanging flower baskets. In the early 1800s, this was the main thoroughfare, headquarters of John Jacob Astor's American Fur Company. It's easy to imagine all the activity that would have occurred on this street in those summers long ago, with Indians, traders, and trappers from the Northwest tramping through.

Up Fort Street stands blinding white Fort Mackinac, the island's historical heavyweight. Constructed during the American Revolution, the British fort finally became the property of the United States in 1796. But during the War of 1812,

the British recaptured the seemingly invincible bastion by attacking from the woods to the north. The Americans failed to regain the fort in a skirmish two years later, but with the end of the war, the Stars and Stripes again waved in 1815. The U.S. War Department closed the fort in 1895. In summer, costumed reenactors fire rifles and cannons to bring the past back to life.

Mackinac Island State Park occupies 81 percent of the island. One great island activity is to rent a bike and pedal into the interior or around the perimeter. It's only eight miles around the island, and a circumnavigation provides a wonderful natural history tour, with trails and picnic spots galore.

With all the bicycles and horses around, one might wonder just how many there are. Answer: nearly 2,000 bikes and 600 horses. They serve a year-round population of 500. The number of people on the island can swell 15 times that on a summer day. Imagine what a different place Mackinac Island would be if all those bikes were cars. . . . On second thought, don't.

A Gift to Be Simple

Surrounded by rolling farmland, tiny Berlin, Ohio, hearkens to a slower, simpler time, when the horse-drawn buggy was the only way to travel and sitting on the front porch with a friend was the best form of entertainment. In Berlin, heart of the world's largest Amish community, you can see how the Amish of eastern Ohio have preserved their uncluttered way of life, and you can sample their wares in craft stores, antique shops, and home-style restaurants.

The Amish gather for meetings, funerals, weddings, and biweekly three-hour church services, held in people's homes and followed by food and socializing. Communion is served only twice a year.

PREVIOUS PAGES: *Wheat sheaves stand ready for hauling to the barn on an Amish farm in Holmes County, Ohio. For 200 years, neatness, thrift, and industry have been the way of life.*

The history of the Plain People here goes back to 1809, when an Amish settler named Jonas Stutzman built a small cabin a few miles east in what is now Walnut Creek. Another pioneer platted the town of Berlin (pronounced BUR-lin) seven years later. More followed, mostly from Pennsylvania, and the settlement grew.

By the middle of the century, most of the state's rural Amish and Mennonite communities had been established. Today about 50 percent of Holmes County's 38,000 residents are of Amish background; the Amish country, which includes several adjacent counties, counts a total of about 80,000 Amish.

The Mennonite Information Center provides more history. The key attraction here is a huge circular mural called Behalt ("to remember") that vividly depicts the history of the Amish and Mennonites from their Swiss origins in 1525 up to the present. The Anabaptist movement, from which the Amish and Mennonites sprang, believed in adult rather than infant baptism. For holding fast to this principle, thousands were put to death. Throughout the centuries, the Amish have cherished their martyrs and kept copious records and letters about them.

On almost every nearby county road today, buggies clip smartly along, driven by men with long beards, traditional straw hats, and dark clothes. On sidewalks and in stores, women in monochromatic aprons and bonnets shop and converse in Pennsylvania Dutch, a mix of German and English. The people driving buggies and wearing old-fashioned clothes are Amish, while many Mennonites are indistinguishable from outsiders.

As a rule of thumb, the Amish are more conservative. The Mennonites in this area are often former Amish who have opted for a modern lifestyle. Most Amish don't drive cars, buy insurance, or use electricity and telephones. They will ride in cars, though, and use gasoline motors on tools and appliances. The idea is that they take care of their own, without reliance upon the outside world.

At Schrock's Amish Farm you can gain more insight into Amish ways. The 150-year-old farmhouse is furnished to reflect both Old Order and New Order Amish lifestyles. Throughout, you'll notice how the house's furnishings embody the Amish people's concern for peace, family solidarity, and humility, which they consider "the most beautiful virtue." There is no television, no electric lights, and no clutter; pictures are limited to scenics, and mirrors are found only in bathrooms. Out back, goats and sheep graze. The barn is redolent of horses and hay.

Visitors tempted to try the Amish life should think hard—very few outsiders have permanently converted, other than those who have married into an Amish family. Giving up modern conveniences is not easy, and the Amish, though friendly, are almost exclusively clannish. Missionaries they are not.

On Berlin's Main Street a country market, a general store, and a few other small businesses reflect the local economy as farmland shrinks and tourism grows. Warm aromas from Der Bake Oven tempt passersby to sample the pies, breads, and cookies for which the Amish are famous. Locals gather at Boyd & Wurthman Restaurant for heaping plates of sausages, Swiss steak, pork chops, mashed potatoes, and green beans, with apple butter and a sauce of peanut butter, marshmallow cream, and karo syrup on the side.

One pleasure of Amish country comes from driving down the country roads, lovely in all seasons, that wind through this pastoral landscape. No shop or town, no matter how delightful, can really compete with long fields of grain and soybeans, late-afternoon light on white farm buildings, and the measured pace of peaceful living. ✎

BERLIN

Each season in Amish country is distinct, with its own charms; autumn's crisp air and colorful foliage are especially appealing. Contact the Amish Country Visitors Bureau (P.O. Box 177, Berlin, OH 44610; 330-893-3467).

MORE ADVENTURES

REENACTING *LITTLE HOUSE ON THE PRAIRIE*

DE SMET

More than a century ago, a little girl named Laura Ingalls moved with her family to the brand-new town of De Smet, in eastern Dakota Territory, to make a home on the vast prairie. Today thousands of people from around the world visit this charming South Dakota community each year, drawn to see the "Little Town on the Prairie" made famous by Laura Ingalls Wilder's books, stories of pioneer life that have become classics. Many things have changed in De Smet since those late-19th-century times, but some things have stayed the same. The formerly empty prairie is now the setting for a town of tree-lined streets and neat houses, where 1,300 live amid great fields of corn and wheat.
Contact: De Smet Chamber of Commerce (605-854-3688; www.travelsd.com).

PLATTE RIVER CROSSROADS

The Platte River, meandering calmly across the Nebraska plains, is actually one of the world's busiest crossroads—for birds. Millions of winged creatures, including a mob of majestic sandhill cranes every spring, stop along a 50-mile stretch of the river and put on a show of soaring, preening, and dancing that draws bird-watchers from all over the world. A century and a half ago, earthbound migrants on the Oregon, California, and Mormon Trails crossed paths here as well and followed the Platte River west. Some pioneers looked around at Nebraska's rippling grasslands and decided they had gone far enough. The prairie whispered its song to writers like Mari Sandoz and Willa Cather, and it still sings to visitors today.
Contact: Kearney Visitors Bureau (308-237-3101 or 800-652-9435; www.kearneycoc.org).

COLUMBUS

Graceful modern buildings designed by the likes of I. M. Pei and Eliel Saarinen, a golf course designed by Robert Trent Jones, Sr., and a lively downtown with 19th-century shopfronts. What major city is this? With 37,000 people, Columbus, Indiana, is barely a city at all. Yet the American Institute of Architects puts only a handful of U.S. cities above Columbus in innovation and architectural design. Like a living laboratory for architecture, this town embraces aesthetics and boasts a self-assured sense of purpose and direction.
Contact: Columbus Area Visitors Center (812-378-2622 or 800-468-6564; www.columbus.in.us).

TWILIGHT AT *EPHRAIM'S EAGLE HARBOR*

EPHRAIM

Summer people consider Ephraim the most desirable among a dozen charming hamlets decorating Wisconsin's Door Peninsula, a 75-mile-long limestone finger pointing northeast across Lake Michigan toward Canada. It holds its harbor in a protective embrace, just as its heritage-conscious citizens protect its oldest buildings, relics of the Norwegians who settled here to farm, log, quarry, and fish. Today, Ephraim is a place to relax—to swim, sail, browse in homey shops, and watch sunsets glow, flare, and fade away above the emerald expanse of Green Bay.

Contact: Ephraim Visitor Information Center (920-854-4989; www.ephraim-doorcounty.com).

REGATTA AT PUT-IN-BAY, OHIO

LAKE ERIE ISLANDS

The magic of an archipelago is that each island can be a world unto itself. The Lake Erie Islands, spaced like skipping stones north of Ohio's Marblehead Peninsula, give visitors a different look at each landfall, from vineyards to bird sanctuaries to a party scene that rivals the Florida Keys. An ecological miracle, Lake Erie now teems with fish and birds only a few decades after pollution threatened to turn it into a watery tomb. Whether you come to cast a line in walleye waters, walk in the woods

looking for warblers, or wassail at a winery, the sight and sound of the lake is never far, and always alluring.

Contact: Ottawa County Visitors Bureau (419-734-4386 or 800-441-1271; www.lakeerie.com).

FANCIFUL PORCH, GALENA, ILLINOIS

GALENA

Tucked away in the northwest corner of Illinois, Galena is one of those secret, special places that snags the heart and captures the imagination. The mists rise from the Galena River, float up the town's tree-shouldered hills, and gently swirl around 150-year-old brick mansions and white church steeples. They seem to hold this remarkable river town in a dreamy, time-blurred spell. From the Ulysses S. Grant Home State Historic Site to the Mississippi Palisades State Park, the town that time forgot is an unforgettable experience for visitors today.

Contact: Galena and Jo Daviess County Convention and Visitors Bureau (815-777-3557 or 800-747-9377; www.galena.org).

CHAPTER 5

Southern Secrets

Silhouetted against a painted sky, fishermen engage in a timeless poling ritual off St. Vincent Island, Florida. The unheralded Apalachicola Coast still has a wild-at-heart feel.

The South

With its mild weather and gentle landscape, there is no place like the South for getting out and about at any time of year. Stepping down from the highlands, the region embraces a vast coastal plain that funnels into the long runway of Florida, dividing the Atlantic Ocean from the Gulf of Mexico. Among its beauties are bird-frequented shores, stream-edged woodlands, and misty blue mountains. But there are also modern cities and charming towns well worth a few days' visit. In this chapter we take you to many of the South's less heralded beauty spots.

In the Miami area you could easily spend a week or more just hanging at the beach. Figuring that anyone can find his way to the sand, we narrow in on the city's art deco and Mediterranean Revival architecture. From southern Florida up to the state's panhandle is a long way, and the untamed coastline up there is a far cry from the sunglasses and beach chairs of Miami. But anyone who thinks

PREVIOUS PAGE: *Point me to the beach, dahling. Polka dots and deco façades are as fashionable in Miami Beach as tankinis and tanned skin. Sun-inspired fun rules on Ocean Drive.*

Florida beaches always mean high-rises and crowds should take a long look at the Apalachicola coast.

In the upper South, we journey to the cradle of rock and roll, on a tour of Memphis blues haunts. And over in eastern Tennessee, there's a small town (the state's oldest) that savvy travelers should put high on their to-do lists. Another small town, Beaufort, North Carolina, makes for a near-perfect mini-getaway. Its Southern coastal history and stately B&Bs give small-town America a good name.

Mountain crafts have become the in thing, and whether you want to make some serious purchases or simply enjoy stopping to chat with local artisans, the journey to Berea, Kentucky, that we have sketched out will get you started. And there's a thumbnail tour of Appalachian crafts in North Carolina, if you happen to be down that way. We also take a peek at some of the finest of the Southern wilderness—Georgia's Okefenokee Swamp and Cumberland Island, the storied hills of Mississippi, and the Potomac highlands of West Virginia.

MIAMI

In Miami, winter is the most comfortable season; in summer, hotel rates drop 20 to 35 percent. Contact the Greater Miami Convention & Visitors Bureau (701 Brickell Ave., Suite 2700, Miami, FL 33131; 305-539-3000 or 800-933-8448; www.miamiandbeaches.com).

Miami Nice

Look beyond the standard-issue skyscrapers of downtown Miami and you'll find one of the country's richest collections of 20th-century buildings. With art deco hotels, Mediterranean Revival fantasies, and an opulent Italian Renaissance villa, Miami opens its arms to fans of fun architecture. As eye-popping now as they were in the 1920s, these vibrant buildings can be enjoyed inside and out. They continue to evoke the flavor of the subtropics—sea breezes, warm sun, and moonlit nights.

Pink stucco, flamingos, and neon went from kitsch to cool in the 1980s, transforming the formerly run-down South Beach area into paradise reclaimed. It also became the capital of all things deco—think 1920s glass brick, bas-relief, and vertical bands of color—but Miami added tropical motifs for its own style. The country's largest deco district—the square mile of Miami Beach circumscribed by the Atlantic, Lenox Avenue, Sixth Street, and Dade Boulevard—encompasses more than 800 art deco and Mediterranean Revival structures.

A good starting point, the 1954 Oceanfront Auditorium now houses the Art Deco Welcome Center. The building at the rear is the 1934 Beach Patrol Station, whose portholes and other ocean-liner stylings typified the "streamline moderne" look of the 1930s (which grew out of deco and its rectilinear designs). Cafés line the main deco strip, Ocean Drive, and one could do worse than simply to have a seat

A lifeguard stand on Miami's South Beach blends well with the colors of sea and sky.
Miami Beach occupies a narrow 7-mile-long barrier island sitting 2.5 miles off the mainland.

and take in the passing parade of the beautiful and strange.

Along Ocean Drive stand numerous small hotels with wonderful deco details, like etched glass and natty nautical motifs. After reaching its heyday in the late 1920s, the deco style here was undone by the Depression and the ensuing construction slowdown in South Florida. Gradually, however, builders began picking up where they had left off. Catercorner from the auditorium, for example, stands the bold blue-and-yellow Breakwater Hotel, boasting a neon sign and terrazzo floors; the building did not go up until 1939.

The 1930 palazzo-style Casa Casuarina was home to designer Gianni Versace until 1997, when he was shot to death on the front steps by suspected serial killer Andrew Cunanan. Just north stand the four delightfully pastel hotels—the Leslie, the Carlyle, the Cardozo, and the Cavalier—that started the wave of restorations in South Beach. Singer Gloria Estefan owns the 1939 Cardozo, designed by noted architect Henry Hofhauser.

An oysterman near Apalachicola, Florida, holds sacks for hauling his catch. The Apalachicola basin claims one of the nation's biggest oyster nurseries, producing some 1,500 tons of meat annually.

Architecture fans will want to reserve half a day or more for Coconut Grove and Coral Gables, classy neighborhoods about 15 minutes from Miami Beach. Miami's oldest settlement, Coconut Grove goes all the way back to the 1870s. The Grove has always attracted an enlightened cross section of society—wealthy industrialists, black Bahamians, hippies, intellectuals. Accordingly, the residential architecture often jumps without warning from simple modern homes to rustic bungalows to urbane mansions. An absolute jaw-dropper of a house, Vizcaya resides in Italian Renaissance–style splendor on sparkling Biscayne Bay. The 1916 mega-villa was designed by Paris-trained, 29-year-old architect F. Burrall Hoffman for industrialist James Deering.

The other essential enclave, Coral Gables, sprang to full life in just five years, as though dreamed into being. One of the nation's first planned communities, it was built during the 1920s Florida land boom. The City Beautiful movement then sweeping the country called for wide, tree-lined avenues, fancy fountains, plazas, and green space galore. Thus did Coral Gables become a fantasy village of tropical pastels, rounded arches, coral-rock loggias, and red-tiled roofs, all set in a hothouse landscape of bougainvilleas, poincianas, hibiscus, and aged vine-wrapped banyans. Though it has mushroomed as a Miami suburb, Coral Gables retains its City Beautiful look— developers receive incentives to conform to the Mediterranean Revival style.

Latitude Adjustment

Those in search of the standard beach vacation will probably not want to bother with a weekend on the Apalachicola Coast. Just where the panhandle bends south, Florida's last undeveloped shoreline is an unpublicized no-man's-land of forest and swampy marshes.

The beaches here are lined with dunes rather than hotels, the barrier islands are wild and deserted, and the only boardwalks are nature trails—not man-made, but pawpaths made by wildlife. Instead of strip malls, there's just the odd fishing village or town. Fun is what you can create for yourself with a river, bay, gulf, and islands. In other words, if you like the real outdoors, there's plenty to see and do here.

On the side of the road near Apalachicola's waterfront stands a little box with a hand-painted sign reading:

GOD IS LOVE
DOG CAFE
FREE EATS
ALWAYS OPEN

The proprietor keeps the box filled with kibble so that no dog will go hungry. That's the way things tend to be in friendly Apalachicola. Almost everyone here (except the watermen) is from somewhere else. They come to visit, to get away—and then they never seem to leave. Life is good at the edge, they'll tell you, easier. Don't worry, be happy. Heck, even be late: The place runs on island time.

Water is the key element here. There's the Apalachicola River, which forms where the Flint and Chattahoochee Rivers meet at Lake Seminole and flows south into shallow Apalachicola Bay. One of the nation's richest estuaries, it is the heart of a great web of rivers, creeks, bays, bayous, marshes, beaches, and barrier islands. Altogether these lands and waters make up the Apalachicola National Estuarine Research Reserve, at 194,000 acres the largest in the country. The diversity of life here is astounding: more than 180 species of fish, at least 300 kinds of birds, some 1,300 different plants, and many mammal, reptile, and amphibian species. Beyond the bays and the barrier islands lies the great, blue Gulf of Mexico.

These rich waters supported the earliest native peoples some 12,000 years ago. Centuries later came Spanish explorers and missionaries, who left the coast its legacy of sainted names. During the 1800s, the river was a major highway for steamboats hauling cotton from Columbus, Georgia, to Apalachicola,

APALACHICOLA

Summer is the most popular season on the Apalachicola Coast, but spring and fall are far more pleasant. Contact the Apalachicola Bay Chamber of Commerce (122 Commerce St., Apalachicola, FL 32320; 850-653-9419; www.apalachicolabay.org).

The Stars and Stripes go up, with the North Carolina flag not far behind, in Beaufort, a charming coastal village with nearly 300 years of history and 100 historic houses, some pre-Revolutionary.

Florida, the Gulf's third largest port. From here, sailing vessels carried the baled cotton off to mills and factories around the world. After the Civil War and the arrival of the railroad, seafood replaced King Cotton as the cash crop. Along the waterfront, where cotton warehouses once stood, you now find seafood plants, shrimp boats, and oyster skiffs. The salty, century-old fishing village of Eastpoint has no-frills local color.

Nature is the real draw along this bend in the coast, though. At its western end, near magnificent Cap San Blas, lies St. Joseph Peninsula State Park, surrounded on three sides by water. To the east sprawl St. Marks National Wildlife Refuge and Edward Ball Wakulla Springs State Park, where you can float above one of the world's deepest springs in a glass bottom boat. In between lie unspoiled barrier island preserves. You have only to cross a bridge to reach St. George Island State Park, a breathtaking expanse of dunes, powdery sands, and blue gulf waters for solitary walking and shelling.

Those seriously thinking of visiting should hurry. There's talk of development,

BEAUFORT

Beaufort has warm summers and damp but mild winters; spring and fall are the best seasons. Contact the Beaufort Historical Association (138 Turner St., Beaufort, NC 28516; 252-728-5225 or 800-575-7483; www.historicbeaufort.com).

and who knows how long this last best coast can resist that tide.

Blackbeard Slept Here

Once disparaged with the name "Fish Town," beautiful little Beaufort (BO-furt), North Carolina, still has an air of working-class sturdiness, despite its renown as an architectural showplace.

Edged up against Taylor's Creek, its perfect grid of shaded streets is blessed by the salty breath of the nearby Atlantic and built chockablock with more than a hundred well-preserved Greek Revival, federal, and Victorian gems, some once owned by yesteryear's sea captains, who inhabited this town. Now turned to B&Bs, the houses seem like town personalities, here long before their current owners and destined to be overseeing Beaufort long after those owners are gone. Like the old-timers, happy to talk with you in their down-home Carolina accent about the Fish Town days, those homes have survived hurricanes, floods, and now an influx of newcomers, who recognize the town's deep-rooted, slow-moving charms.

Far from the roar of traffic and similar travails, Beaufort wakes up to the sounds of garden birds twittering and gulls cawing out along the creek edge. The streets are still quiet at nine o'clock, though a few old men might be gathered on porch steps or at storefronts to talk over the issues of the day—the fishing season, recent prize catches, sports news, and the like.

In the early 1900s the waterfront of Beaufort, North Carolina, bustled with longshoremen working wooden sailing vessels. Fishing continues, but tourism takes top place in today's economy.

PREVIOUS PAGES: *Sun spangles the waters of Beaufort Harbor, from which pirate Blackbeard harrassed ships in the early 1700s. Whatever treasure he hoarded has never been found.*

Morning is a good time to stroll through Beaufort's Old Burying Ground. Nestled beneath lordly live oaks and lush resurrection ferns, most of the tombstones in the walled and crowded space face east, toward the rising sun. Since the early 1700s, this was the coveted place for your days to end, and such town fathers as Josiah Bell rest in peace here, along with many who died in the Revolutionary and Civil Wars.

But the town's roots go far back beyond them. The Coree Indians had their own village—Cwarioc (Fish Town)—on these banks long before Europeans arrived. In 1713 the earliest settlers carefully laid out the streets of the old village, declared it a seaport, and named it for the Duke of Beaufort. As a local historian wrote, "It is not unusual to find that nearly everyone who was born and bred here is related." That robust pride in roots is most obvious at Beaufort Historic Site, a clutch of buildings in the heart of town.

Docents decked out in colonial mobcaps and flocked skirts take great pleasure in leading tours through the six collected historic structures, a few still standing where they were built. The docents relate in detail the grisly doctoring techniques of centuries past, how houses were built to withstand hurricanes, and how the town has changed over time.

Another big draw in this little town is the North Carolina Maritime Museum, which traces the coastal commerce of the state back from the modern fish and shellfish industries to the shore-whaling that went on in these waters in the past. Probably the museum's most romantic exhibit is the one on Blackbeard, privateer extraordinaire. The region's pirating legacy has drawn archaeologists to an underwater site not far off the coast where they have located Blackbeard's ship, dubbed *Queen Anne's Revenge.*

The museum displays cannons and other artifacts from that ship, which sank off the coast here in 1718.

When you have exhausted the town's museums, the beaches are waiting. Water taxis ferry people out across the creek to windswept Carrot Island and Shackleford Banks, where you can walk the wide beaches and picnic in utter peace. The ferry will get you back in town in time to catch the sunset over generous dinners of seafood, lamb, or beef at the Spouter Inn, right on the waterfront. Another local favorite, Beaufort's Grocery Store Company, serves fresh, innovative seafood in a setting as welcoming as an old general store.

Picking and jawing, banjoist Don McConnell performs at the National Storytelling Festival in Jonesborough, Tennessee. Since 1973 the festival has grown from an audience of 60 to more than 10,000, all eager to hear tall tales, mountain yarns, and good old-fashioned stories.

PREVIOUS PAGES: *Oh, the stories it could tell: Jonesborough's oldest, the 1793 Rees-Hawley House was solidly built of dovetailed chestnut logs on a native limestone foundation.*

As Old as the Hills

Set in the picturesque hill country to the east, the oldest town in the state of Tennessee is a time capsule of early America. From the top of Main Street, you can behold dozens of restored, early-19th-century brick buildings, punctuated by the white spires of churches. Shop fronts and sidewalks sport seasonal decorations, while locals and tourists alike rest on benches outside the courthouse. Jonesborough combines country style with polish, and its pulse is easy to take. A weekend getaway at one of the many elegant B&Bs can quickly restore you to a saner rhythm and revise your concept of small-town Appalachia.

Jonesborough has only come into its own within the last few decades. The raw material was always there—historic buildings, pioneer heroes, and a pleasant setting—but by the late 1960s, a slow economy and the sprawling growth of nearby Johnson City started drying up Jonesborough's fortunes.

Then two things happened. Citizens got their town listed on the National Register of Historic Places, a first for the state, and in 1973, the National Storytelling Festival

JONESBOROUGH

Pleasant to visit in spring or summer—or in fall, for the Storytelling Festival. Contact the Historic Jonesborough Visitor Center (117 Boone St., Jonesborough, TN 37659; 423-753-1010; www.jonesboroughonline.com).

was born here. It has become an annual event. Some local merchants claim the festival generates almost half their income for the year.

On the small but thriving downtown, lampposts and brick sidewalks lend an air of times gone by. Buildings sport large windows, ornamental cornices, and a large concentration of stepped gables. Founded in 1779 as a county seat in western North Carolina, Jonesborough five years later became the capital of the breakaway state of Franklin. But after a brief battle, the town returned to the fold and became part of Tennessee when the new state was formed in 1796. Andrew Jackson was a judge here; Davy Crockett was born about ten miles away; Daniel Boone hunted in the woods nearby.

Jackson, the town's most prominent early citizen, stayed at the Chester Inn. The rambling 1790s building, with a breezy second-floor veranda, also hosted two other presidents, James Polk and Andrew Johnson. It now houses the offices of Storytelling Foundation International, with exhibits and an auditorium. The national revival of the oral tradition is due in part to the annual October weekend, which draws some 10,000 participants and listeners to Jonesborough every year.

Another ancient structure, the Rees-Hawley House, is documented as the "oldest house in Tennessee's oldest town." It operates as a B&B and is open for tours if you call ahead. The original chestnut log structure, dating from 1793, was

Rock and roll came wailing into the world at tiny Sun Studio in Memphis. Early stars who cut records here include Elvis Presley, Jerry Lee Lewis, Carl Perkins, B.B. King, and Muddy Waters.

augmented with a frame addition and wide front porch. Painstaking attention to historical accuracy is evident in the furnishing and restoration, and it is typical of the care given to old houses throughout Jonesborough. Friendly B&B hostess Marcy Hawley supplies visitors with details on the house and the town— historic and current.

At the end of the day, Jonesborough locals and visitors alike head to the Cranberry Thistle, a delightful den of flavored coffees, healthful sandwiches, and delicious cakes and brownies. This is the place to catch up on the latest gossip and news. Whether the discussion centers on the rezoning of a street or on something said by somebody's grandfather in

church one day, you'll find yourself at the heart of small-town America here.

Recent years have seen the steady return of people who had grown up in Jonesborough, left town, and then thought the better of it. Perhaps people need to go away to appreciate the quality of life, one member of the historic zoning commission says. "Since I've been here, I've never lost my keys, because I leave them in the car, and there's no key to the house," she says. She has a neighbor who walks her dog at two o'clock in the morning, hearing only the rumble of trains and the chiming of the courthouse clock. The price for such freedom is relative isolation, but more and more people are thinking that's not a bad price at all.

Elvis busts for sale: The myth and the mania never die at Graceland, the neoclassic mansion outside Memphis that Elvis Presley bought at the age of 22 for $100,000 cash. He furnished it with a mirrored staircase, wall carpeting, and an indoor waterfall, and died there in 1977. On Memphis's Beale Street, opposite, the riffs and howls of blues spill into the night.

Memphis legend B. B. King plays his guitar, named Lucille. Born in 1925, King worked on a cotton plantation and sang gospel in church before he gained fame as the greatest blues guitarist ever.

Memphis Blues

Rock and roll was born and bred in Memphis, Tennessee. This journey charts the past and present of that music in the city's lively, revitalized downtown. Here

MEMPHIS

Spring and fall are the best times to visit Memphis. Contact: Memphis Convention & Visitors Bureau (47 Union Ave., Memphis, TN 38103; 901-543-5300 or 800-873-6282; www.memphistravel.com).

you can visit fine museums and a thriving entertainment district full of blues and rock clubs. Farther out there's Graceland, home of musical and cultural icon Elvis Presley.

Downtown Memphis perches on the east bank of the Mississippi River, directly across from Arkansas to the west and just a few miles north of Mississippi. This was the site of the merger of three musical styles—the country music of whites, the blues of Delta and urban blacks, and the gospel songs of both cultures. Then the blend picked up a driving beat and became rock and roll.

The story of that fusion is told in riveting detail at the Memphis Rock 'n' Soul Museum. Researched and organized by the Smithsonian Institution, the museum's recordings and memorabilia present as a theme the crossroads of music and culture. Visitors may don headsets and listen to dozens of historic recordings by musicians from country star Roy Acuff to bluesman Robert Johnson to soul legend Otis Redding. Hearing them all would take hours, but you can pick your favorites and listen to as much of each as you like.

Sun Studio is the place where early blues bands recorded rock and roll's first great hits. Here in the 1950s, owner Sam Phillips produced recordings of Howlin' Wolf, Johnny Cash, and Roy Orbison. A young Memphis truck driver cut a record entitled "That's All Right" at Sun Studio in 1954, and the music world was never the same. His name was Elvis Presley.

A tour of Sun Studio consists of little more than standing in the place where hits such as "Great Balls of Fire" were made, learning about studio history, and listening to recordings. For true fans of rock and roll, however, that's plenty.

The appeal of Memphis music is not exclusively historical. The entertainment district around Beale Street encompasses several blocks of restaurants, shops, and rock and blues clubs showcasing the sort of talent that still flocks to the city. Just about any night here, there's great music at spots such as B. B. King's Blues Club, Isaac Hayes, and Rum Boogie Café. B. B. King once worked as a disc jockey at Memphis radio station WDIA, where he

was known as the "Beale Street Blues Boy" (hence his double initials). The legendary singer-guitarist appears at his club several times a year, with tickets selling out well in advance.

On Elvis Presley Boulevard in southern Memphis stands one of America's most visited homes: Graceland. The King lived in this white-columned 1930s mansion for 20 years, and he died here in 1977. The residence reflects Elvis's unique taste in interior design: pleated fabric walls, three televisions playing simultaneously, white faux-fur bed, and indoor waterfall. Personal memorabilia include Presley's costumes for stage and movies, his many gold records (worldwide sales estimated at one billion), his jewelry, and his guns.

Additional Elvis attractions await across the street. An auto museum displays a Ferrari and his famed pink Cadillac. Also on the tour is one of his customized jets.

Broomsticks & Bluegrass

Tucked into the Cumberland foothills, where Kentucky's bluegrass brushes up against the mountains, the little town of Berea claims a big reputation. As folk arts and crafts capital of the state of Kentucky, the town acts as a kind of year-round fair of woodwork, ceramics, weaving, wrought iron, broomcraft, and other handcrafted creations.

Some hundred artisans sell their work in forty galleries scattered about town. As if that weren't enough, three major annual crafts festivals draw on talent from around the region and the nation.

Berea College's elegant white-columned Boone Tavern Hotel, an institution since 1909, serves up country ham, spoon bread, Jefferson Davis pie, and other regional specialties.

PREVIOUS PAGES: *Warp and woof of tradition: A weaver works loom magic at Berea College. Kentucky's capital of folk art, Berea holds some 40 shops and studios, run by independent artisans.*

But the heart of the community lies in historic Berea College, where many students continue to learn traditional Appalachian crafts.

The tree-shaded campus of Berea College has no intimidating maze of buildings and streets. The enrollment here is a mere 1,500, so parking and walking are a breeze. It's worth noting, though, that Berea has been ranked among the very top liberal arts colleges in the South.

In 1853 abolitionist Cassius Clay donated a tract of land in what was then called the Glade to establish a base for his antislavery movement. Despite a shaky start, the tiny village of Berea held on, and the forerunner of Berea College opened in 1855, offering admission equally to blacks and whites, men and women.

That unprecedented egalitarianism did not sit well with the state legislature, which passed a law in 1904 forbidding interracial education. The college then focused its efforts on educating less fortunate whites from the mountains. Some of the students paid tuition with handmade coverlets, and to capitalize on the growing

national interest in Appalachian culture, the school began marketing handmade crafts. To this day: All students are on full scholarship, working 10 to 15 hours a week in crafts studios or as employees in other college-run facilities. Together with Asheville, North Carolina, Berea has been a leader in the revival of American crafts, beginning in the late 1920s.

You'll see student workers across Main Street at the white-columned Boone Tavern Hotel of Berea College. Built in 1909, this gracious southern hostelry is a great place to lean back in a student-made, cane-bottomed chair for a spell, or to take a meal in an elegant dining room. Boone Tavern anchors College Square, home to a number of shops and restaurants.

One worthwhile stop is Warren May's. For over 25 years, May has been turning cherry, walnut, poplar, and other local woods into exquisite furniture. But he is best known for his elegant dulcimers. Those who listen to him play often end up plunking down $300 to buy one.

The nearby Log House Craft Gallery sells the best of handcrafted pieces. They don't offer bargains; the pieces here reflect expert work. Brooms with walnut handles, wrought-iron candelabras, and stools made of woven sea grass are a few of the items for sale here—while in the weaving cottage and the broomcraft and woodcraft shops out back, students ply their talents at mountain crafts. ⟡

BEREA

Berea is at its best in spring and autumn. Contact Berea Tourism Center (201 N. Broadway, Berea, KY 40403; 859-986-2540 or 800-598-5263; www.berea.com).

MORE WHISPERS

AMERICAN ALLIGATOR, OKEFENOKEE SWAMP

SWAMP TO SEA

There are few wild places left where you can find true solitude. Two of them—the Okefenokee Swamp and Cumberland Island—lie in southern Georgia. Situated one hundred feet above sea level, the vast Okefenokee contains great, dark swaths of primordial cypress swamp and alligator-infested bayous. Discover its lighter side, too: lakes filled with floating islands, flooded prairies and acres of open pinelands. Just 40 miles east, Cumberland—Georgia's largest and southern-most barrier island—is a subtropical jungle of maritime forest fringed by wide dunes and white beaches, where wild horses, deer, and armadillos roam amid the ruins of crumbling mansions. Both island and swamp have their stories to tell.

Contact: Okefenokee National Wildlife Refuge (912-496-7836; www.fws.gov/okefenokee) and St. Marys Tourism Council (866-868-2199 or 912-882-4000; www.stmaryswelcome.com).

HILLS OF MISSISSIPPI

The hills of Mississippi may seem a geographical oxymoron, like the beaches of West Virginia, but they're as real as the flat cotton fields that out-siders usually imagine when they think of the Magnolia State. In the extreme northeast rise the Tennessee River Hills, honest-to-goodness high-lands that represent the southwesternmost extension of the Appalachians. Occupying a broad belt through north-central Mississippi are, appro-priately enough, the North Central Hills, a red-dirt landscape covered in mixed pine and hardwood forest and intersected by rivers and creeks. Lovely state parks, antebellum mansions, the Natchez Trace Parkway, and the home of writer William Faulkner make this area a worthwhile jaunt.

Contact: Mississippi Tourism (866-733-6477; www.visitmississippi.org).

STUDENT SMITHS, NORTH CAROLINA

APPALACHIAN CRAFTS

In the mountains west of Charlotte, craftsmen and -women have been turning out beautifully executed works of art for centuries. The region now holds one of the largest concentrations of crafts makers in the country, with over 160 studios, more than 100 galleries, scores of museums, and two well-established crafts schools. One can spend a delightful weekend rambling the back roads, learning about contemporary crafts, and seeking out that perfect objet d'art to bring home and cherish.

Contact: Southern Highland Craft Guild (828-298-7928; www.southernhighlandguild.org).

BARTER THEATRE, ABINGDON, VIRGINIA

ABINGDON

As the sun sets on the misty blue landscape of southwest Virginia, sending long shadows on tree-carpeted mountains and velvety pastures, all is quiet—except in the little highland town of Abingdon, where the Barter Theatre is in full swing. Whatever the play, you can bet its production will be first-class, for the Barter is the State Theater of Virginia, and it remains the home of one of the oldest, still extant professional resident acting companies in America. But there's more to Abingdon than theater: Genteel B&Bs, candlelit restaurants, boutiques, artists' studios, a four-star historic hotel, and a wonderful rail trail all combine to create a vibrant destination deep in the heart of the southern Appalachians.

Contact: Abingdon Convention & Visitors Bureau (276-676-2282 or 800-435-3440; www.abingdon.com; www.bartertheatre.com).

ALMOST HEAVEN

Embracing a swath of the Monongahela National Forest along the eastern border of West Virginia, the region from Seneca Rocks to Lewisburg is a special place for outdoorspeople both resident and visiting. Poet William Blake wrote, "Great things are done where man and mountain meet," and here, recreationists agree. The dramatic landscape is the attraction, the lights are celestial, and the cacophony of great rivers provides the background music for it all. Mountains rise in rows across the horizon, each riven by tiny clear streams. Cascading down hollows and valleys, the creeks rasp the mountainsides, building to swift, strong currents along the valley floors and feeding the five major river systems draining this area.

Contact: West Virginia Division of Tourism (304-558-2200 or 800-225-5982; www.callwva.com).

MONONGAHELA NATIONAL FOREST

Chapter 6

Yankee Landscapes

Weekends across the Northeast take in attractive small towns like Sunderland, Massachusetts,

THE NORTHEAST

S teeped in early American history and brimful of scenes worthy of a canvas, the Northeast has so many weekend escape possibilities that you would be hard pressed to see them all in a lifetime. The region from Pennsylvania to Maine certainly claims an extensive variety of terrain. Not even the northeastern seacoast is all of a piece: Rolling Atlantic breakers shape the broad, sandy barrier beaches of Cape Cod, while calmer waters lap the shores of Long Island Sound, and the pounding surf perpetually hammers the rocky coast of Maine. Inland, the low country of exurban New England, won from the forest by colonial axes, still remains a patchwork of rolling meadows. To the west the hills grow higher, becoming true mountains in Pennsylvania's Appalachians and New York's Adirondacks, along Vermont's green cordillera, in the fastnesses of northern New Hampshire where Mount Washington reigns amid its own often frightening weather, and on the lonely massif of Mount Katahdin in Maine, surrounded by a silent ocean of pine.

PREVIOUS PAGE: *Gravestones lean shoulder to shoulder at the Church on the Hill in Lenox, Massachusetts. Such peaceful Berkshire scenes have inspired generations of artists and writers.*

We settle into the northern Maine backwoods in a place we call the Land of the Moose, where abundant wildlife still roams in a dense forest reminiscent of 1800s America. Down in southern Rhode Island we investigate an area of cozy seaside villages awash in early colonial lore. Lying to the west, the Berkshires of Massachusetts are rich in American literaray associations, having served as a getaway and home for the muses who inspired Hawthorne, Melville, Wharton, Thoreau, and others.

On the tip of Long Island, the unpublicized fishing village of Cutchogue, New York, wears well the sheen of 350 years, enticing visitors with local wines, lobsters, and potatoes. The forested Laurel Highlands have survived their industrial heritage and come out full of wonders, including an American architectural masterpiece. Down in delightful Bucks County, north of Philadelphia, the rural lifestyle is an art form, preserved in painterly landscapes, art studios, and village greens. We end by mentioning other destinations, from collegial Hanover, New Hampshire, to Pennsylvania's historic Brandywine Valley.

> ## MAINE
> Visit northern Maine from spring through fall. Contact the Moosehead Lake Region Chamber of Commerce, Greenville, ME 04441 (207-695-2702, 888-876-2222; www.mooseheadlake.org).

Land of the Moose

Not all of America's frontier country lies in Alaska, or in the great roadless spaces of the Rocky Mountains. Much of northern Maine has the look and feel of a place settled yesterday—and, in parts, not settled at all. Between Rockwood and The Forks, where the mighty Kennebec River spills out of Moosehead Lake and roils through a logging and sporting empire, the terrain still has a rugged look. After all, this is territory that belongs to the loon, the bear, and, most of all, the lordly moose.

In the 1780s the Commonwealth of Massachusetts held a lottery of unsettled land in its northernmost province—a wilderness called Maine, which had few inland inhabitants and another quarter-century to go before it would achieve statehood. A Philadelphia banker named William Bingham drew several townships in the lottery and bought out the rest, thus becoming master of two million acres. Half of that land lay along the upper reaches of the Kennebec River, west and south of Moosehead Lake.

Lumbermen began clearing Bingham's domain soon after he acquired it. Down came the stands of giant white pine prized for ships' masts during colonial days. Thankfully, the woods grew back fast and, although lumbermen are still at it, grand, silent—albeit second-growth—forests still cover much of this northwestern part of the state. Rivers once choked with logs being funneled downstream now support another industry—adventure vacations. From early May through mid-October,

Belly-deep in the Maine woods, a bull moose munches aquatic vegetation. Moose can swim for up to two hours and stay submerged for half a minute to escape black flies and to forage underwater.

whitewater-rafting enthusiasts head for a stretch of the upper Kennebec River between The Forks and Moosehead to begin a 12-mile run through secluded forest and a deep, rock-walled gorge.

Moosehead Lake, heart of this hidden corner and gateway to a wilderness domain stretching to Baxter State Park, the Allagash Wilderness Waterway, and Canada, is the largest lake in New England contained within one state: It's 35 miles long and 10 miles across at its widest point. Much of the shoreline is publicly owned and retains its primitive character; beyond lie miles and miles of unbroken forest and views ranging as far as distant Mount Katahdin. Opposite Rockwood, Mount Kineo rises dramatically out of the water. Attached to land by way of a peninsula, the sheer-face flint peak is the haunt of bald eagles and peregrine falcons. Here, along the Indian Trail, hikers can follow in the footsteps of Native Americans who once climbed to the summit to peer across the wilderness and chip flint for weapons and tools.

Family fishing in the sun-gilded surf gets high ratings in Rhode Island's South County, nickname for the coastal parts of Washington County, one of five counties in the state.

PREVIOUS PAGES: *Maine's highest peak, 5,267-foot Mount Katahdin reflects on Sandy Stream Pond in Baxter State Park. The Appalachian Trail has its northern terminus here.*

Like its rivers and lakes, Maine's forests are appreciated nowadays for more than their commercial value. The burgeoning moose population attracts riflemen—as well as outsiders armed with cameras. The Moose River and Moosehead Lake regions are among the Northeast's most popular spots for moose watching. The Moosehead Lake Region Chamber of Commerce even provides a "moose sighting" map, and several businesses around the lake offer seasonal "moose cruises" to observe moose and other wildlife, including bears, eagles, peregrine falcons, and ospreys.

Some might say that the area is downright moose-crazy. In Greenville, the month-long Moosemainea festivities begin each May. Moose and their young can be seen everywhere—especially in the early morning and at dusk, when they come out to feed. Other

Moosemainea events include moose meat tastings, moose-calling competitions, and a Tour de Moose mountain bike race.

Painter's Dream

Lake-pocked and ocean-washed, southern Rhode Island stays low to the earth—a flat, intimate landscape that begs exploration and attracts its own colony of artists. Here you can catch glimpses of history out of the corner of your eye—shades of Native Americans and colonial celebrities, such as Roger Williams and portraitist Gilbert Stuart. But present-day personages fill most scenes with vitality, what with busy beaches, popular inns, quaint villages, and the hallowed halls of the University of Rhode Island.

Wedged between the neighboring state of Connecticut and the Atlantic Ocean, this southern square of Rhode Island is far quieter than the environs of capital city, Providence, to the north, or the state's famous mansion town, Newport, to the east, across the waters of Narragansett Bay. As the bay sweeps up the coastline here, it breaches the land, filigreeing the area with marshes, creeks, and narrow rivers. The wetlands give way to state park beaches in the south end, as the bay broadens to meet Rhode Island Sound.

The first white man to recognize the quiet appeal of this coastal landscape was none other than Roger Williams, founder of the colony. Warned that he was about to be banished by the Massachusetts Puritans for his views, considered blasphemous, he fled south in 1636 to the lands around Narragansett Bay. In 1637 he established a trading post here,

bartering with the Narragansett Indians for beaver furs. He later sold his trading post lands to partner Richard Smith, and today the restored Smith's Castle stands on the same site, overlooking a lovely stretch of Wickford Harbor. Once a New England saltbox-style clapboard, the house has gone through style changes, but the earliest portions took shape in 1678, a couple of years after the Great Swamp Fight wreaked havoc across the area.

The fighting began in 1675, when about a thousand colonial troops gathered on Smith's lands and readied themselves to do battle against the local Indians. Seeing trouble coming, the Indians had taken shelter in the Great Swamp, about a dozen miles to the southwest. In a pitched assault, the colonists massacred them. The swamp, now a marshy woodland, shows no signs of the battle save a few modern historical markers. The colonists themselves suffered about 200 casualties, and 40 of them were buried in a mass grave at the edge of Smith's Castle.

A couple of miles away, the lovely village of Wickford wraps itself around a small, reedy harbor. Incorporated in 1674, it is now an upscale mecca, with stylish boutiques and alfresco restaurants that attract weekend guests. The venerable

SOUTH COUNTY, RHODE ISLAND

In South County, spring and fall are great for bird-watching; beaches make prime summer getaways. Contact the South County Tourism Council (4808 Tower Hill Rd., Wakefield, RI 02879; 401-789-4422 or 800-548-4662; www.southcountyri.com).

No skin exposed: In 1914 parasols, long skirts, and white gloves were the fashionable look at social events held at South County's Narragansett Pier, such as a Point Judith Club polo match.

1707 Old Narragansett Church claims the distinction of being the oldest Episcopal Church north of the Mason-Dixon line.

The atmosphere changes dramatically down the coast in the town of Narragansett, once a fashionable Victorian watering hole and now a brawny, condominium-framed beach resort. A few mementos of the elegant past have survived, however: the long, strollable Narragansett Pier and the twin stone Towers, once part of a renowned casino designed by McKim, Mead & White and now a museum to commemorate that era.

As the southern coast opens up onto Rhode Island Sound, its sandy verge is protected by one state beach after another. At the biggest of these, Scarborough State Beach, you may have to squeeze your blanket in among the weekend crowds, but the breezes and cool ocean waters make it all worthwhile.

The town of Westerly glistens with stately Victorian houses and a lively and growing arts community. Painters, actors, and musicians flock to the town, particularly in summer, when all kinds of concert and theater series are ongoing. The area's setting is inspiring, from the fountained gardens of Wilcox Park to the white sand beaches and Victorian cottage mansions of nearby Watch Hill. With nostalgia floating in the air, you can get yourself an ice cream cone, stroll along Little Narragansett Bay, and enjoy the lost art of living gently.

Literary Heroes 101

The wild beauty of the Berkshires, a hilly, remote corner of western Massachusetts, has inspired writers and artists for more than a century. Herman Melville, Edith Wharton, and Norman Rockwell all became enchanted with the area's dreamy mountain vistas, its pine-scented woods, and its white-steepled villages full of Victorian charm. The stomping grounds of these personalities offer a glimpse of their creative quests.

On a summer day in 1850, local writers Nathaniel Hawthorne and Herman Melville climbed 1,750-foot Monument Mountain for a picnic. A sudden thunderstorm drove them into a cave and sparked a friendship that lasted a lifetime. One can now follow in their footsteps along a quintessential New England trail that ambles beneath a mantle of hemlocks, white pines, and oaks before summiting the mountain, magnificent views all around. The fall is an especially beautiful season, with tulip poplars and maples exploding in vibrant hues.

Nearby Stockbridge epitomizes New England charm. The village is probably

THE BERKSHIRES

Summer is high season in the Berkshires; in spring and autumn, tourist crowds are lighter. Contact the Berkshire Visitors Bureau (3 Hoosac St., Adams, MA 01220; 413-443-9186 or 800-237-5747; www.berkshires.org).

best known as the longtime home of illustrator Norman Rockwell, who lived off Main Street from 1953 to 1978. His trademark painting, "Stockbridge Main Street at Christmas," shows the town center in snowy, festive splendor. The painting hangs in the Norman Rockwell Museum, home to more than 200 works by the prolific 20th-century illustrator.

Practically next door, sculptor Daniel Chester French purchased a country estate in 1896 and named it Chesterwood. The setting was sufficiently scintillating to inspire the artist for the next 34 summers: French's home and studio commands, as he put it, "the best dry view" he had ever seen. Here he put the finishing touches on such masterpieces as the central seated figure for the Washington, D.C., Lincoln Memorial, completed in 1922.

Stockbridge's centerpiece is the historic Red Lion Inn. To stay here is to step into a Rockwell painting. The inn's charms include flowery wallpaper, Staffordshire china, and an enormous veranda where people watching is a venerable tradition. Begun in 1773 as a stagecoach stop on the road from Boston to Albany, the Red Lion also features a couple of restaurants with classic New England cuisine.

Embodying the cultural Berkshires, Lenox is the shining star of the Gilded Age, situated about eight miles north of Stockbridge. Here some of the world's finest writers—among them Nathaniel Hawthorne, Herman Melville, and Edith Wharton—retreated to be inspired by the cool, woodsy breezes. They joined New York's and Boston's genteel elite, whose summer "cottages," as they called their grand vacation homes, gave the area the feel of an inland Newport. The 1929 crash turned easy street into a dead end, but many of the mansions have been reborn as inns or B&Bs. Combining two old estates, Tanglewood has been the summer home of the Boston Symphony Orchestra since 1937. In addition to its splendid views over the hills, Tanglewood offers classical, jazz, and pop music concerts by world-famous performers.

Also in Lenox stands one of the region's most elegant mansions, The Mount, the former residence of author and social satirist Edith Wharton. Wharton built her palatial cottage in 1902, and there she wrote her 1905 bestseller, *The House of Mirth*. Baroque rooms overlook the estate's Italian-style gardens, their spaces seming to echo the lazy afternoon conversations that must have taken place between Wharton and her sophisticated guests, including her close friend and mentor, Henry James.

Rising high above the northern Berkshires' remote landscape, 3,491-foot Mount Greylock is distinctive from all directions. Its summit, which takes in five states, has been a moody muse for writers, artists, and romantics through the ages. Henry David Thoreau described a sunrise from the top as "Aurora playing with the rosy fingers of the Dawn, and not a crevice through the clouds from which those trivial places of Massachusetts, Connecticut, and Vermont could be seen."

At the Hancock Shaker Village in Pittsfield, Massachusetts, above, visitors learn about the Shaker virtues of simplicity, pacifism, and equality of gender and race. Further outdoor pleasures await in nearby Lenox, below, home of Tanglewood, the oldest music festival in the country.

Daylight dies on Long Island Sound, tempering the beach near Cutchogue on tranquil North Fork. New York City feels far away here, where locals make a living off oysters, potatoes, and grapes.

Catching Cutchogue

Leave New York's traffic jams, noise, and congestion behind as you head east along Long Island's quiet North Fork, a thin strip of land surrounded on three sides by water. Local residents have long made their livings off the land and the sea. Tiny Cutchogue is a typical village here, its main road dotted with wineries, farm stands, and antique shops. Its back roads wind down to Long Island Sound and the sea, offering visitors a hidden world of tidal estuaries and shallow creeks teeming with birds and marine life.

Throughout Cutchogue's 350-year history, its fortunes have ebbed and flowed like the tides of Peconic Bay and Long Island Sound, which border it. Over the years its people made their living scalloping, oystering, crabbing, and potato farming. Then, in the early 1970s, Alex and Louisa Hargrave planted a crop that changed the face of Cutchogue, as well as much of the rest of the East End's North Fork. Following in the footsteps of Moses Fournier, who operated a thriving vineyard here in colonial times, they planted 17 acres of their former potato farm in Cabernet Sauvignon grapes. Today 6 of the North Fork's 21 vineyards are in Cutchogue, and the potato has been eclipsed by the grape.

One reason vineyards thrive on the North Fork is the sandy soil, which permits excellent drainage. The other reason is what has made Long Island's East End a tourist mecca for many years: The island has about 220 days of sun each year, the most of any place on the northeastern seaboard. Until recently, most vacationers had flocked to upscale South Fork resorts such as the Hamptons and Montauk. But now they're discovering that tiny towns like Cutchogue, along Long Island's North Fork, offer more tranquil—and often less costly—alternatives.

First-time visitors to Cutchogue often get so caught up in winery-hopping that they forget the town has many other fascinating places to explore. When the first Europeans, a small band of Puritans, arrived on the North Fork in 1640, they were greeted by the Corchaug Indians, who had settled here many years before and had built a sturdy fort on present-day Downs' Creek, just southwest of the village. Today's inhabitants of the fort site include numerous species of waterfowl, such as ospreys, green herons, and egrets. A migratory flyway, the estuary attracts bird-watchers throughout the year. The Corchaug harvested whelk and clam shells here to make wampum. The waters are still a good spot to go clamming today.

Cutchogue's oldest house—and one of the oldest in the state—was built five miles down the road in Southold, in 1649, by an English immigrant, then moved

CUTCHOGUE

Cutchogue is lovely all year round. Contact the North Fork Promotion Council (Box 1865, Southold, NY 11971; 631-298-5757; www.northfork.org).

White with snow, Cutchogue's village green holds the 1649 Old House—a National Historic Landmark—as well as other historic buildings. Grapes ripen at Corey Creek Vineyard, opposite, one of half a dozen Cutchogue vineyards. In a tasting room nearby, vineyard visitors can sample the fruits of the vine: Chardonnay, Gewurtztraminer, and Merlot.

Cantilevered terraces of architect Frank Lloyd Wright's Fallingwater hover above a 20-foot waterfall in Pennsylvania's Laurel Highlands. The 1930s house integrates design with nature.

piecemeal to its present site in 1660. Today The Old House, a national historic landmark, anchors a complex of buildings on the village green.

LAUREL HIGHLANDS

The Laurel Highlands are lovely at all times of year, although winters can be cold and snowy. Contact the Laurel Highlands Visitors Bureau, Ligonier, PA 15658 (724-238-5661 or 800-925-7669; www.laurelhighlands.org).

Wickham has long been a popular name in these parts: Three generations of Wickhams lived in The Old House. Today their descendants own Wickham's Fruit Farm, just the place to pick up supplies for a picnic lunch. Another might be Braun's Seafood Company, the East End's leading distributor of seafood. The company processes as much as 100,000 pounds of fresh fish and 30,000 lobsters each week in summer. It also boils shrimp and lobster to go.

If you're looking for potatoes, you can find farmers who still grow the famous

Long Island spuds. And if you're looking for an East Coast answer to Napa Valley, you've come to the right place, too. Add striking seascapes and colorful local history, and you're in for a wonderful escape.

The Wright Place

Pocketed in the Allegheny Mountains, the Laurel Highlands of southwestern Pennsylvania tumble along in wooded ridges and dipping vales cut by fast-flowing creeks. Though the steel towns of the rust belt surround them, a gentle beauty prevails here. Old inns stand beside long-forgotten stagecoach routes, a famous white-water river races beneath lacy hemlocks, and the architecture of Frank Lloyd Wright crowns forested bluffs.

The quiet simplicity of the Laurel Highlands today gives little hint of their storied past. Long before 19th-century industrial barons of nearby Pittsburgh discovered the highlands, others recognized their worth—particularly as a gateway to the coveted Ohio River Valley to the west. As early as 1754, a regiment of Virginia Frontiersmen was dispatched to this area to protect British colonial interests from French encroachment.

The commander of the small group was an untested, 22-year-old lieutenant colonel named George Washington. Soon enough he was put to the test—and found up to it. At Fort Necessity National Battlefield, you can learn of Washington's bravery. He launched a surprise attack on the French and yet, despite his efforts, had to surrender to forces who outnumbered him almost two to one. It was the first defeat of Washington's career, and he and nearly all his men were allowed to walk away from the battle.

A year later Washington was back, as an aide to British Maj. Gen. Edward Braddock. Braddock's formal style of fighting proved little good in the wilds of America, and he was mortally wounded in battle. He died near Fort Necessity. Nearby, the 1828 Mount Washington Tavern details the glory days of the National Road, as US 40 was designated. Built in the early 1800s, it was the federal government's first foray into road building.

The footprints of past skirmishes rest easy now on these Appalachian Highlands. In the centuries since Washington's war, other structures more appealing than rustic colonial forts have risen in the once contested quarter—two of them by architect Frank Lloyd Wright. Cosseted amid poplar, oak, and wild rhododendron, the Wright-designed house called Fallingwater is, as one critic rhapsodized, "one of the complete masterpieces of twentieth-century art." Designed to jut out over a small waterfall in the creek, the house actually seems to be part of the landscape.

Wright was in his late sixties in 1936 when Edgar Kaufmann, a Pittsburgh millionaire, asked him to design a country home. Its intimate interior forces the eye outside to the natural surroundings. Fallingwater immediately won kudos from architectural critics, but today the structural weaknesses in Wright's design are beginning to show. The cantilevered terraces may now be in danger of falling,

Whaling boats and Conestoga wagons cram the four-story atrium of the Mercer Museum in Bucks County's Doylestown. Eccentric Henry Mercer built the museum for his own collection.

and unappealing shorings have been placed under them temporarily. Still, Fallingwater has lost no mystique.

Another Wright home in the area opened to the public in 1996. Wright designed modest but elegant Kentuck Knob in 1953 for local ice cream entrepreneur I. N. Hagan. The great gaping gorge that the house overlooks provides more than just visual stimulation. It is one of the main draws in the area, particularly for white-water fans, who flock here to run the Yough (pronounced YOCK)—the Youghiogheny River. About 14 miles of gorge is protected within the 19,000 acres of Ohiopyle State Park, and the rustic little town of Ohiopyle, deep in the gorge, is replete with white-water outfitters, guides, and endless talk of treacherous Class IV rapids.

The only real city in the area, Johnstown, Pennsylvania, is wedged into a perilous bowl created by steep-sided hills. In this working town of rust belt vintage, the smokestacks of the steel industry still rise like yesteryear's sky-scrapers, and the nostalgic Johnstown Inclined Plane still carries cars and people up its steep slope.

The town is best remembered for the tragedy of May 31, 1889. Heavy spring rains put pressure on the lake's neglected South Fork Dam, and it gave way. "A roar of thunder," as eyewitnesses called it, shook the area as 20 million tons of water hurtled into Johnstown. When it was all over, more than 2,200 people lay dead. An Academy Award–winning film at the Johnstown Flood Museum recounts

the horror. The Great Johnstown Flood became a symbol of the tragic side of industrial success.

Bucks County Palette

Creativity is a way of life in Bucks County, Pennsylvania. Attracted by country lanes, green hillsides, charming old bridges, and remnants of rural tradition, countless painters, writers, and craftspeople have sought inspiration in this farm-dappled county along the Delaware River just north of Philadelphia. After a weekend in central Bucks, it's easy to see why.

Doylestown is a lovely little burg whose intimate downtown resembles the set of an old-time movie. Its bookstores and small shops are a good place to start exploring Bucks County. On the outskirts of town lies Fonthill, a modern concrete masterpiece and the dream home of Henry Mercer. Locally born and educated at Harvard, the relentlessly inquisitive Mercer abandoned the legal profession to pursue the study of archaeology and anthropology and to satisfy his passion for the world's best arts and crafts.

BUCKS COUNTY

Bucks County is fine all year round. Inns fill early for fall foliage season. Contact the Bucks County Conference & Visitors Bureau (3207 Street Rd., Bensalem, PA 19020; 888-359-9110 or 800-836-2825; www.buckscountytourism.org).

Continental soldiers head to the Delaware River in a reenactment of the dramatic river passage of December 25-26, 1776, at Washington Crossing Historic Park in Bucks County, Pennsylvania.

PREVIOUS PAGE: *Small enough to be friendly and easy to visit, sophisticated enough to offer nightlife with its own charm, Doylestown typifies Pennsylvania's Bucks County.*

Completed in 1912, Mercer's castle home is one of a kind: 44 unique rooms connected by a disorienting maze of serpentine staircases and claustrophobic passageways. Painted tiles cluster along walls and pillars, cling to the ceiling, and encircle the windows. Many of the tiles were fashioned next door at the Moravian Pottery and Tile Works. In this cloistered, mission-style building, Mercer developed his fascination for handcrafted ceramics, turning his home into a famous—and highly profitable—business.

Across the street, the James A. Michener Art Museum is housed in the former county prison. Founded around the collection of the prolific author, the museum features many local paintings that demonstrate the role of impressionism in Pennsylvania art. A breathtaking Japanese-style room also highlights the region's artistic diversity.

Northwest of town lies the Pearl S. Buck House and Historic Site. It was in the stone farmhouse on this 60-acre estate that Buck wrote her most famous book—*The Good*

Earth, a bestselling novel about Chinese peasant life, made into a play and a movie. Buck received both the Pulitzer Prize and the Nobel Prize for Literature—first American woman to win the latter. A passionate humanitarian, Pearl Buck's legacy continues through international adoption and education missions operated in association with her house.

Bucks County still thrives on arts and crafts. Art galleries, craft stores, shops, and boutiques all line the streets of New Hope, a small riverside town northeast of Doylestown. Many galleries sell paintings by current Pennsylvania impressionists, working artists taking inspiration from painters of the early 20th-century .

The best way to see Bucks County's natural beauty is to parallel the Delaware on River Road—one of the Northeast's prettiest riverside drives. North of New Hope, you'll find a rolling road dotted with inns, old bridges, and shadowed, narrow side roads that beckon.

Just south of New Hope lie the shady trails of Bowman's Hill Wildflower Preserve. Throughout the year, these one hundred leafy acres are spangled with the glorious colors of Pennsylvania's native plants in bloom, a thousand species in all. From the top of Bowman's Hill, there's a delicious view of Bucks County: Fields and farms spread out below in a colorful panorama worthy of a painter's canvas. ✑

Doylestown native Henry Mercer built his concrete castle without blueprints. Mismatched windows, disappearing stairways, and narrow passages show his flair for the unorthodox.

More Postcards

HANOVER

On a fine, crisp New Hampshire day, this stately college town, set on a high plateau above the east bank of the Connecticut River, is within viewing distance of Vermont's Green Mountains and the soaring massifs of the White Mountains. Its 9,000 residents celebrate educational excellence, taking great pride in world-renowned Dartmouth College, the prime feature of the town. Hanover possesses an air of academic aloofness coupled with the charm of a neoclassic campus enveloping an enormous green, the focal point of the community. The place radiates culture, with its theater and galleries offering an array of soul-nurturing delights.

Contact: Hanover Area Chamber of Commerce (603-643-3115; www.hanoverchamber.org).

DARTMOUTH COLLEGE, HANOVER, NEW HAMPSHIRE

CUTTYHUNK ISLAND

Westernmost of the Elizabeth Islands, Cuttyhunk lies lazily in Buzzards Bay, unaffected by the hubbub going on at its chic nextdoor neighbor, Martha's Vineyard, or back on the southern Massachusetts mainland just 14 miles away. Vacation homes, old and new, terrace its low slopes, making it look like a Mediterranean hill town. In summer the

population swells from the year-round average of 30 hardy souls to an impressive 300 or so, thanks to urban escapees. Any time of year, though, here you can find yourself an isolated, rock-ribbed beach, sit back in the sun, and forget that there is a world beyond.

Contact: New Bedford Office of Tourism and Marketing (800-508-5353; www.ci.new-bedford.ma.us).

CUTTYHUNK ISLAND ICE CREAM PARLOR

CENTRAL ADIRONDACKS

Cold, stream-fed lakes framed by bowers of spruce and cedar; dense, verdant forests; rolling meadows blanketed in wildflowers; placid blue water dotted with coves and islands; and Gilded Age estates, known as great camps: All of these would top the fantasies of a feudal lord, and all are hallmarks of the central section of New York State's Adirondack Park. An officially protected area, the park sprawls across the northern one-fifth of New York State's landmass. At six million acres, it is larger than the entire state of Massachusetts.

Contact: Adirondack Regional Tourism Council, Pittsburgh, NY 12901 (518-846-8016 or 800-487-6867; www.adk.com).

COLD SPRING

Up New York's storied Hudson River lies a town that loomed large in colonial times and during the Revolutionary and Civil Wars. Although the U.S. Military Academy at West Point stands just across the river, Cold Spring has long since beaten its swords into plowshares and become a favorite weekend retreat for antique lovers and enthusiasts of Hudson Valley lore.

Contact: Cold Spring/Garrison Chamber of Commerce (845-265-3200; www.coldspringchamber.com).

OYSTERMEN IN BIVALVE, NEW JERSEY

DOWN JERSEY

The Delaware River arcs against the southern coast of New Jersey, its marshes seeping inland in a slow, steady melding of land and sea. Life here in "Down Jersey" moves more to the tides than to any human rhythm, though the waves of human history have brushed quickly over this place, then moved on. In their wake, they left behind some captivating remnants of a prosperous colonial past. Once this coastline supported lively summer resorts—some now no more than ghost villages on stilts—and a clam and oyster industry, still memorialized in high white mounds of shell.

Contact: Bridgeton-Cumberland Tourist Association (800-319-3379; www.njsouthernshore.com).

BRANDYWINE VALLEY

The ambitious and resourceful du Pont family established an industrial empire in this lush river valley along the Pennsylvania-Delaware border during the 19th century. The powder-mill smoke dissipated long ago, and today the Brandywine Valley offers a surprising wealth of art and architecture; artists have long sought inspiration here, including renowned illustrator Howard Pyle, his student N. C. Wyeth, and subsequent generations of Wyeths as well. Estates, gardens, and museums attract both those who create beauty and those who admire it.

Contact: Chester County Conference and Visitor Center (610-280-6145 or 800-228-9933; www.brandywinevalley.com).

LONGWOOD GARDENS, CHESTER COUNTY

FURTHER JOURNEYS

*For those who journey to the places
in this book, we provide a list of
other nearby places to enrich your stay.*

Chapter 1
FURTHER JOURNEYS ON THE WEST COAST

WHEN YOU'RE IN PORT TOWNSEND

Victoria Inner Harbour, British Columbia
72 miles northwest of Port Townsend, via
Highway 101 and the Port Angeles ferry
250-414-6999
http://www.tourismvictoria.com
Some 20 whale-watching tours depart from
Victoria's Inner Harbour each day in hopes of
catching glimpses of the orca whales in waters
nearby from mid-spring to mid-fall.

Naval Memorial Museum of the Pacific
Bremerton, 50 miles south of Port Townsend on
Highway 3
360-479-7447
Open since 1954, this museum contains
artifacts from naval history including a
Korean bamboo-wrapped cannon dating
from 1377, and Puget Sound naval
memorabilia. Nearby, visitors can also
tour the historic USS Turner Joy, a 1959
destroyer that saw action in the Gulf of
Tonkin during the Vietnam War.

WHEN YOU'RE ON THE VOLCANO TRAIL

Bonneville Fish Hatchery
Bonneville Lock and Dam, about 60 miles
southwest of Mount Adams on I-84
541-374-8820
http://www.nwp.usace.army.mil/op/b/home.asp
Maintained by the U.S. Army Corps of Engineers,
the hatchery provides Chinook salmon a ladder
for successful upstream mating. Visit rearing
ponds and learn how salmon spawn.

**Chimpanzee and Human Communication
Institute**
Ellensburg, about 90 miles east of Mount Rainier
National Park on U.S. 12 and I-82
509-963-2244
http://www.cwu.edu/~cwuchci/
Attend a chimposium—a one-hour workshop
in which visitors meet CHCI's world-famous
chimpanzees, expert in using American Sign
Language. Scientists consider their work not
entertainment but research and education, so
reservations and a fee are required.

Yakima Valley
About 100 miles east of Mount Rainier on I-82
http://www.winesnw.com/yak.html

Pastels stripe a landscape looking out over Orcas Island, Washington.

More than 40 wineries abound in this area, which was Washington State's first approved and award-winning viticultural region. Many of the wineries are open to the public, but at some, reservations are required.

WHEN YOU'RE IN SEASIDE OREGON

Evergreen Aviation Museum

McMinnville, about 50 miles east of Lincoln City on Highway 18
503-434-4180
www.sprucegoose.org
Home to Howard Hughes's Spruce Goose, the Blackbird SR-71, and a Russian space capsule, this museum displays more than 50 other historic cargo, passenger, and bomber planes—and exhibits aeronautical artifacts as well.

Astoria Column

In Astoria, at the mouth of the Columbia River
http://www.oregoncoast.com/Astorcol/Astorcol.htm
Climb the 164-step spiral staircase inside an intricately painted 125-foot tower for views of Mount Rainier, Mount St. Helens, the Columbia River, and the Pacific. Atop Coxcomb Hill, the column is built on the site of the first permanent white settlement west of the Rockies.

WHEN YOU'RE IN THE HIGH DESERT

Diamond Craters

About 55 miles southeast of Burns on U.S. 205
http://gorp.away.com/gorp/activity/byway/or_dcrat.htm
A geologist's dream, wild and remote, with features including lava flows, domes, pits, craters, rimrock, and Malheur Maar, a springfed lake. Diamond Craters has been called an on-site museum of basaltic volcanism. Tank up on gas and water beforehand, because there are no amenities in Diamond Craters.

WHEN YOU'RE IN THE SAN DIEGO BACKCOUNTRY

Twentynine Palms Oasis of Murals

On Highway 62 between I-15 and I-10, 57 miles east of Palm Springs
760-361-2286
www.oasisofmurals.com
For more than a decade, Twentynine Palms's thriving artist community has been painting the sides of city buildings. Now there are at least 20 murals. Subjects range from local characters such as longtime bus driver Johnnie Hasty to desert flash floods of the 1940s.

WHEN YOU'RE IN MONTEREY BAY

The National Steinbeck Center

Salinas, 17 miles from Monterey
831-796-3833
http://www.steinbeck.org
In Historic Old Town Salinas, the Steinbeck Center combines a museum and a memorial. Seven theaters highlight novelist John Steinbeck's works. Exhibits and activities feature him and the many facets of his California home that come through in his writing.

Chapter 2
FURTHER JOURNEYS IN THE WESTERN STATES

WHEN YOU'RE IN LAS VEGAS

Hoover Dam

30 miles southeast of Las Vegas on U.S. 93, on the Arizona/Nevada border
http://www.usbr.gov/lc/hooverdam/
Don't just drive over it; stop and learn more about this engineering marvel. The dam's two-hour tour includes a gaze at the massive generators and a stroll across the overlook. Open in summer only, 9 a.m. to 6 p.m.

LA MISIÓN DE SAN MIGUEL, PATAGONIA, ARIZONA

Lake Mead Cruises

Just off Lakeshore Road/Highway 166, Boulder
City, about 30 miles southeast of Las Vegas
702-293-6180
http://www.lakemeadcruises.com
Before there was a Hoover Dam, there was
beautiful Lake Mead. Get to know this
natural landscape by taking a narrated one-
hour cruise on the lake at the foot of the
colossal dam, April through October.
Reservations recommended.

WHEN YOU'RE AT GRAND STAIRCASE

Kodachrome Basin State Park

North edge of Grand Staircase–Escalante National
Monument, 9 miles south of Utah Route 12
435-679-8562
http://www.stateparks.utah.gov/park_pages/scenic
parkpage.php?id=kbsp
Drive or hike through the park to view the
famed pipes towering here—actually, solidified
geysers—as well as sandstone chimneys, red rock
formations, and quiet desert beauty.

Bluff, Utah

On U.S.163/191, 26 miles south of Blanding and
45 miles northeast of Monument Valley
http://www.go-utah.com/Bluff
The place where the ancient basket maker
and the cliff dweller tribes met, Bluff is a
small town set against a spectacular redrock

canyon backdrop. Burial sites, petroglyphs,
and abandoned buildings tell the ancient
story. Navajos from the adjacent reservation
help bring the story up to the present day.

WHEN YOU'RE IN NORTHERN ARIZONA

John Wesley Powell Museum

On U.S. 89 in Page, south of Arizona-Utah border
928-645-9496
www.powellmuseum.org
Honoring Civil War veteran Powell and his 1869
and 1871 Colorado River longboat expeditions,
this museum also offers Native American and
pioneer artifacts together with documentary films
on Lake Powell and local history. It's a good
starting point for Colorado River rafting trips.

Goulding's Lodge Museum

Monument Valley, just north of Arizona/Utah
border on U.S. 163
435-727-3231
www.gouldings.com
This museum, restaurant, campground, and
lodge calls itself a gateway into Navajoland. At
night, a photographic Earth Spirit Show is dis-
played. In day, depart from here for Monument
Valley, Canyon de Chelly, and the Four Corners.

WHEN YOU'RE IN PATAGONIA

Tombstone, Arizona

About 50 miles east of Patagonia on Highway 82
888-457-3929
http://www.cityoftombstone.com/
A mining camp gone outlaw, Tombstone was
home to Doc Holiday, Big Nose Kate, Wyatt
and James Earp. Local history museum in an
1882 building chronicles the life of this quintessential Wild West town. Includes gallows, jail
cell, and restored courtroom. Witness the
famous showdown at a reconstructed OK
Corral, reenacted every afternoon at 2 p.m.

Biosphere 2

About 30 miles north of Tucson on Highway 77

32540 S. Biosphere Rd., Oracle, AZ 85623

520-838-6200

http://www.bio2.com

High-tech structure of steel and glass encloses 7.2 million cubic feet of the Sonoran Desert in a 1980s effort to create a sealed replica of the Earth's environment. A crew of eight lived inside for two years, from 1991 to 1993. Now visitors can take an under-the-glass tour to see their world, including a 900,000-gallon ocean, a rain forest, a desert, farmland, and human habitats, together with an exhibition on global climate change.

Historic Nogales

On the Mexican border, off Highway 82, about 20 miles southwest of Patagonia

520-287-4621

http://www.nogalesmainstreet.com

Main Street meets Mexico in this town proud of its history, from Spanish missionary Fray Marcos de Niza to Mexican independence fighter Pancho Villa. Pimeria Alta Museum, in the 1914 town hall, recounts the history.

WHEN YOU'RE IN THE COLORADO ROCKIES

South Park

Near Fairplay on Colorado Route 9, just north-west of I-285, a 60-mile drive from Leadville

719-836-2387

www.southparkcity.org

Just south of the Hoosier Pass and nothing like the TV show, South Park is in a designated Colorado Heritage Area and offers a 32-building re-creation of a 19th-century gold-mining town. Nearby Como celebrates its railroad past with an 1880s stone-and-wood roundhouse, while Alma, a mining ghost town, sits near glistening Kite Lake, altitude 12,400, surrounded by taller peaks.

WHEN YOU'RE IN SOUTHWEST MONTANA

Elkhorn Hot Springs

Polaris, south of Dillon on I-15, then west on State Route 278 to Pioneer Scenic Byway

406-834-3434

www.elkhornhotsprings.com

Outdoor pools hold water up to 100°F while two indoor pools offer a wet sauna up to 106°F. Lodge available, but passersby can take the waters, too, in this rustic mineral springs log cabin resort surrounded by two million acres of national forest. Limited access in winter.

Big Hole National Battlefield

Ten miles west of Wisdom, Montana, on Highway 43

406-689-3155

http://www.nps.gov/biho

They fled their homeland and crossed east into Montana Territory, refusing to move onto a reservation. Then, at this site, a village of about 750 Nez Perce Indians was attacked on an early August morning, 1877. Remember the Nez Perce War of August 1877 with a visit to Big Hole National Battlefield, incorporating part of the four-state Nez Perce National Historical Park.

Chapter 3
FURTHER JOURNEYS IN THE SOUTH-CENTRAL STATES

WHEN YOU'RE IN SAN ANTONIO

Gruene Hall

About 30 miles north of San Antonio

1281 Gruene Road, New Braunfels, TX 78130

830-606-1281

www.gruenehall.com

You've got to love a town whose motto is "Gently resisting change since 1872." Gruene Hall, built

SPRING JAZZ FEST, NEW ORLEANS

in the 1880s, claims to be the oldest Texas dance hall. Live night music summer and winter.

New Braunfels Museum of Art and Music
About 30 miles north of San Antonio on I-35
1257 Gruene Road, Gruene, TX 78130
830-625-5636 or 800-456-4866
http://www.nbmuseum.org/musinfo.htm
An affiliate of the Smithsonian Institution, this vibrant cultural center emphasizes folk art and music, crafts, and decorative arts of the American Southwest. It sponsors constantly rotating exhibits and schedules many concerts and programs throughout the year.

WHEN YOU'RE IN EAST TEXAS
Tyler Municipal Rose Garden Museum
On U.S. 69 just south of I-20 in Tyler
420 Rose Park Dr., Tyler, TX 75702
903-597-3130
www.texasrosefestival.com/
Rosebushes numbering nearly 40,000 and representing 500 varieties grow on these 14 acres of city land. The museum holds artifacts of Texas's rose-growing history and Tyler's annual rose festival. The garden includes a trial area where new varieties are evaluated before marketing.

Cherokee Trace Drive Thru Safari Park
About 33 miles northwest of Caddoan on U.S. 69
1200 C.R. 4405, Jacksonville, TX 75766
903.683.3322
www.cherokeetrace.org
More than a dozen exotic and endangered animals call this 300-acre open savannah preserve home, situated in settings designed to replicate their native environments.

Old Stone Fort Museum
20 miles north of Lufkin on Texas Route 59
Griffith Boulevard at Alumni Drive
Stephen F. Austin State University
Nacogdoches, TX 75962
www.visitnacogdoches.org
Located in the oldest town in Texas, the Old Stone Fort is sometimes called the Alamo of East Texas. Three attempts to launch Texas as its own republic were made here.

WHEN YOU'RE IN NEW ORLEANS
The Mardi Gras Museum
About 14 miles west of New Orleans on I-10
415 Williams Blvd., Rivertown, Kenner, Louisiana
504-468-7231
www.rivertownkenner.com/mgmus.html
Enjoy demonstrations on making floats and costumes, exhibits and videos on the King Cake, society balls, French Quarter history, the legendary parades, and Cajun Acadiana.

WHEN YOU'RE IN EUREKA SPRINGS
Beaver Lake
About 10 miles west, Highway 62 to 187S
2260 North 2nd Street, Rogers, AR 72756
479-636-1210
www.swl.usace.army.mil/parks/beaver
More than 480 miles of shoreline with a dozen campground parks, many hiking trails, swimming beaches, boat launches, and cruise opportunities.

WHEN YOU'RE IN THE MISSOURI RHINELAND

Graceland Museum

About 60 miles northwest of Hermann on
U.S. 40 Audrain County Historical Society
501 S. Muldrow , Mexico, MO 65265
573-581-3910
www.audrain.org

Built in 1857 and used by Colonel Ulysses S.
Grant during the Civil War, this midwestern
mansion now treats guests to the elegance of
Victorian-era Missouri. The nearby American
Saddlebred Horse Museum celebrates the area's
long reputation for saddle horses.

August A. Busch Memorial Conservation Area

About 70 miles east of Hermann on I-70
2360 Highway D, St. Charles, MO 63304
636-441-4554
www.conservation.state.mo.us/areas/cnc/busch

Explore 7,000 acres of self-guided trails and
enhance your explorations by enrolling in outdoor
skills classes offered here.

WHEN YOU'RE IN THE FLINT HILLS

Fort Leavenworth

On the base, north of Highway 92, near the
Missouri border
Frontier Army Museum
100 Reynolds Ave., Fort Leavenworth, KS 66027
913-683-1724
garrison.leavenworth.army.mil

Visit the oldest fort west of the Mississippi and see
wagon ruts left by pioneers on their travels. The
museum also displays artifacts of the lives of
soldiers based here between 1804 and 1917.

Santa Fe Trail and Flint Hills Scenic Byway

212 W Main St, Council Grove, KS 66846
620-767-5882 or 800-732-9211
www.councilgrove.com

Start at Council Grove's Main Street and proceed
on an 18-stop journey along the Santa Fe Trail
and Flint Hills Scenic Byway.

Chapter 4
FURTHER JOURNEYS IN THE MIDWEST

WHEN YOU'RE IN THE LAND OF LEWIS AND CLARK

Garrison Dam

South end of Lake Sakakawea, just east of Pick City
Riverdale, North Dakota 58565
701-654-7411
www.nwo.usace.army.mil/html/Lake_Proj/
garrison/dam.html

Built on the Missouri River, the Garrison is one of
the world's largest rolled earth-fill dams. Daily
tours of the dam and its power plant are offered
at noon and 3 p.m. in the summer.

Crazy Horse Memorial

In Black Hills, SD, on U.S. 16/385 ,17 miles
southeast of Mount Rushmore
Avenue of the Chiefs, Crazy Horse, SD 57730
605-673-4681
www.crazyhorse.org

The world's largest sculpture, begun in 1948 and
still in progress, designed to memorialize Crazy
Horse, the Lakota warrior crucial to the Indian
victory over George A. Custer at the Little
Bighorn. Site includes Indian Museum of North
America, with art, artifacts, and narratives.

WHEN YOU'RE NEAR THE MISSISSIPPI HEADWATERS

Giant Paul Bunyan and Babe statues

Bemidji, Minnesota 56619
800-458-2223 ext. 105 , 218-759-0164
www.visitbemidji.com

Wood and canvas statues 18 feet tall, built in

CARRIAGE RIDE, MACKINAC ISLAND, MICHIGAN

1937, mark this town as Paul Bunyan's birthplace. Also see the Fireplace of States, built with stones from every state and province.

Cut Foot Sioux Trail

In the Chippewa National Forest on Highway 46, about 18 miles northwest of Deer River
www.fs.fed.us/r9/chippewa
Follow a trail, 22 miles long, that tracks Minnesota's Continental Divide. From here, water flows north to Hudson Bay, east to the Great Lakes, and south to the Mississippi. From the same starting point, take the 13-mile Simpson Creek trail for eagle, osprey, and loon viewings.

WHEN YOU'RE IN THE AMANA COLONIES

Herbert Hoover Presidential Library-Museum

About 11 miles west of Iowa City on I-80
319-643-5301
www.hoover.archives.gov
Hoover's birthplace and gravesite, plus his father's blacksmith shop, a frontier schoolhouse, Quaker meetinghouse, and library holdings of notable Americans including the manuscripts of Laura Ingalls Wilder. Surrounded by about 80 acres of prairie land.

National Motorcycle Museum

About 50 miles northeast of Amana on U.S. 151
200 E. Main St., Anamosa, IA 52205
319-462-3925
www.nationalmcmuseum.org

Ogle more than 170 motorbikes, dating back to the 1880s. The museum includes a replica motorcycle service store from the early 1900s, an engine exhibit, and the Motorcycle Hall of Fame.

WHEN YOU'RE IN CHICAGO

Ernest Hemingway Birthplace and Museum

Oak Park, 10 miles west of downtown Chicago
200 N. Oak Park Ave., Oak Park, IL 60301
708-848-2222
www.ehfop.org
Hemingway's 1899 birthplace. Stately Victorian home with large turret and wrap-around porch in the leafy, elegant suburb of Oak Park. Museum displays many of the author's journal, letters, and manuscripts.

Archicenter

In the historic Santa Fe building, across from the Art Institute
224 South Michigan Avenue, Chicago, IL 60604
312-922-3432
http://www.architecture.org
Departure point for more than 75 different guided tours. Explore Chicago's architecture and neighborhoods on foot or by boat, bus, train or bicycle from here. Atrium gallery features new architectural designs. CitySpace offers rotating exhibits. Lecture hall and learning studio.

Chicago Cruise Lines

North Pier Docks, McClurg Ct. and Illinois St., between Michigan Ave. and Lake Shore Dr.
480 N. McClurg Ct., Chicago, IL 60604
312-527-2002
http://www.chicagoline.com
Cruise on Lake Michigan for a guided tour of Chicago's history. Cruise the Chicago River for the best views and an informative tour of the city's architecture. Refreshments are included on these 90-minute journeys.

WHEN YOU'RE ON MACKINAC ISLAND

Colonial Michilimackinac

On Mackinac Island

P.O. Box 873

Mackinaw City, MI 49701

231-436-4100

http://www.mackinacparks.com/parks/colonial-michilimackinac_7/

Reconstructed 1715 French fur-trading outpost. Reenactments, costumed guides, archaeology exhibit, and more, all to evoke the world that early white settlers found and built here.

Soo Locks

Portage Avenue, Sault St. Marie, MI

800-647-2858 (800-MI-SAULT)

http://www.soolocksvisitorscenter.com

Thousand-foot-long freighters travel the Great Lakes thanks to the five Soo Locks, first built in 1855 and still in use commercially today. Walk the bridges and passageways or take a cruise boat through the locks.

WHEN YOU'RE IN BERLIN, OHIO

Pro Football Hall of Fame

About 30 miles northeast of Berlin on U.S. 62

2121 George Halas Drive NW, Canton, OH 44708

330-456-8207

www.profootballhof.com

Celebrate America's favorite pastime in the birthplace of the American Professional Football Association, now the National Football League.

Historic Roscoe Village

About 28 miles south of Berlin on Highway 83

381 Hill Street

Coshocton, OH 43812

740-622-9310

www.roscoevillage.com

Visit this restored 1830s port town on the Ohio and Erie to get a sense of the importance of the

canal two centuries ago by riding the horse-drawn Monticello III canal boat.

Chapter 5
FURTHER JOURNEYS IN THE SOUTH

WHEN YOU'RE IN MIAMI

The Venetian Pool

Located in Coral Gables, about 6 miles southwest of Miami on U.S. 1 and I-95

2701 DeSoto Blvd., Coral Gables, FL 33134

www.venetianpool.com

This world-famous springfed pool was built in the 1920s from a coral rock quarry and includes nature and culture: grottoes, coral caves, waterfalls, and elegant Italian tile decor.

WHEN YOU'RE IN APPALACHICOLA

Micanopy Historical Society Museum and Thrasher Warehouse

Micanopy, FL 32667

South of Gainesville, just east of I-75

352-466-3200

There's not much of old Florida left, but Micanopy is considered the state's oldest inland town. Founded in 1821 and named for a Seminole chief, the town boasts 39 sites on the National Register of Historic Places.

Marjorie Kinnan Rawlings State Historic Site

Between Ocala and Gainesville east of I-85

18700 S. Country Road 325, Cross Creek, FL 32640

352-466-3672

www.floridastateparks.org/marjoriekinnanrawlings

The Florida-cracker–style home of Marjorie Kinnan Rawlings, author of the 1938 Pulitzer Prize winner, The Yearling. Farm, citrus grove, and nature trails around the house evoke rural Florida in the 1930s.

BEALE STREET, MEMPHIS, TENNESSEE

WHEN YOU'RE IN BEAUFORT, NORTH CAROLINA

Somerset Place

From US 17, take US 64 east to Creswell, just south of Albemarle Sound

2572 Lake Shore Road, Creswell, NC 27928

252-797-4560

http://www.albemarle-nc.com/somerset/

Antebellum North Carolina comes to life at this historic estate, an active plantation from 1785 and one of the Upper South's largest by 1865. Once home to some 300 enslaved African Americans, this 100,000-acre farm grew rice, corn, and wheat.

WHEN YOU'RE IN JONESBOROUGH, TENNESSEE

Barter Theater

In Abingdon, Virginia, about 50 miles northeast of Jonesborough on I-26 and I-81

127 West Main Street, Abingdon, VA 24212

276-628-3991

www.bartertheatre.com

The official State Theater of Virginia, this landmark first opened during the Depression, when theater goers bartered farm produce for a seat. Performances are staged in the historic theater and in an intimate, innovative thrust stage. Across the street is the Martha Washington Inn, a former girls' school and Civil War hospital dating to 1832.

Grove Park Inn

About 60 miles south of Jonesborough on I-26

290 Macon Ave., Asheville, NC 28804

828-252-2711

www.groveparkinn.com

A 1913-built granite luxury hotel with 510 rooms and stunning views of the Blue Ridge Mountains. Its Great Hall glows with 14-foot stone fireplaces.

WHEN YOU'RE IN MEMPHIS

Country Music Hall of Fame

In Nashville near exit 209A off I-40

22 Fifth Ave. S., Nashville, TN. 38502

615-416-2001, 800-852-6437

www.countrymusichalloffame.com

Sights and sounds tell the history of the music at the heart of America. Hear recordings, interactive displays, and videos on the country music's roots and future directions.

WHEN YOU'RE IN BEREA

Fall Creek Falls State Park

Off Highway 111, 16 miles south of Spencer, Tennessee

423-881-5241, 800-250-8610

www.uppercumberland.org/outdoors.htm

Swinging bridge offers the best view of this park's magnificent waterfall. At 256 feet, it plummets farther than Niagara Falls and is the highest falls east of the Rockies.

Historic Homesteads Tower Museum

Junction of I-27S and U.S. 68

Crossville, Tennessee

931-456-9663

www.tnvacation.com/vendors/homesteads_tower_museum

Memorializing one of Franklin D. Roosevelt's New Deal accomplishments, this museum showcases the 250-home experimental community built here for local subsistence farmers.

Chapter 6
FURTHER JOURNEYS IN THE NORTHEAST

WHEN YOU'RE IN MAINE
Maine Lobster Museum
On Highway 3 west of Bar Harbor
Mount Desert Oceanarium
3829 Route 3
Bar Harbor, ME 04609
207-288-5005
theoceanarium.com/oceanbhsite.html
Visit a lobster hatchery to get up close and personal with these remarkable creatures. Especialy good for kids, with its hands-on opportunities to understand the lobster life-cycle. Open mid-May through October.

Vinalhaven Island
In Penobscot Bay, 13 miles off Maine's midcoast
207-863-4471
www.vinalhaven.org
Rugged island, settled in the 1760s, hosting one of the U.S.'s largest lobster fleets. Swim in chilly, clear quarries once the location of a thriving granite industry. Ferries travel from Rockland, on the mainland, to Vinalhaven all day long.

WHEN YOU'RE IN SOUTH COUNTY, RHODE ISLAND
Blackstone River Valley
Visitors Center at 175 Main St., Pawtucket, opposite City Hall
Blackstone Valley Tourism Council
401-724-2200
www.tourblackstone.com
Every waterfall and tributary of this 46-mile-long river once powered a mill. Explore by bicycle, car, or canal boat, and be sure not to miss Blackstone Gorge. To orient yourself, start your explorations at Visitors Center in Pawtucket.

Lowell National Historical Park
From Boston, 30 miles northwest on U.S. 3
Morgan Cultural Center and Boardinghouse
978-970-5000
www.nps.gov/lowe/
Pick up your time card, tie on work apron, and report for your shift at the Boott Cotton Mills Museum to experience what life was like for immigrants and "mill girls." This is one of several sites at the park memorializing Lowell's famous textile industry.

WHEN YOU'RE IN THE BERKSHIRES
Lake Waramaug State Park
Near New Preston and north of New Milford, Highway 202 to State Route 45
860-868-0220
dep.state.ct.us/stateparks/parks/lakewaramaug.htm
Lake Waramaug curves through a landscape gentle on the eyes, spectacular for fall colors but pleasing in every season. Inns and wineries welcome visitors. A total of 77 camping sites surround the pristine lake.

Sharon Audubon Center
25 miles northwest of Torrington on Highway 4
860-364-0520
www.audubon.org/local/sanctuary/sharon/
Eleven miles of hiking trails through more than a thousand acres of mixed forest, meadows, wetlands, ponds, and streams. Trails are well marked; choose between the Woodchuck Trail, the Fern Trail, the Bog Meadow Trail, and more.

WHEN YOU'RE IN CUTCHOGUE
North Fork
Northeast tip of Long Island, 90 miles east of Manhattan
Long Island Convention and Visitor's Bureau
877-386-6654
www.licvb.com

BUCKS COUNTY, PENNSYLVANIA, FESTIVAL

Taste wine at Castello di Borghese/Hargrave Vineyards, one of the oldest of the many wineries on the North Fork. Find great views of Long Island Sound at the Horton Point Lighthouse, bike or swim at Orient Beach State Park, visit Cutchogue's Old House on the Village Green along with other preserved homes dating back to 1649.

WHEN YOU'RE IN THE LAUREL HIGHLANDS

Cooperstown, New York
About 70 miles west of Albany, on Highway 28 off I-88
607-547-9983
www.cooperstownchamber.org
There's more to Cooperstown than the famous National Baseball Hall of Fame. This is the family home of author James Fenimore Cooper, whose spirit inspires the local Farmers' Museum, which brings the 19th-century Fenimore Farm back to life, and the Fenimore Art Museum, focusing on Native American and early American art.

Long Island Heritage Trail
Route 25A, stretching 100 miles from Great Neck to Port Jefferson
516-751-2244
www.newsday.com/extras/island/heritagetrail/

Remember East Egg and West Egg from F. Scott Fitzgerald's classic novel? Scott and Zelda Fitzgerald lived in Great Neck, memorialized in *The Great Gatsby* as West Egg. They looked longingly east at Port Washington, a more upscale community—Jay Gatsby's East Egg in the novel—and now home to the Science Museum of Long Island. Continue east to Stony Brook/Setaucket to view homes from the 1700s.

WHEN YOU'RE IN BUCKS COUNTY, PENNSYLVANIA

Pine Barrens
South from I-195, east from I-295, in southeastern New Jersey
NJ Pinelands National Reserve
609-894-7300
www.nps.gov/pine; www.pineypower.com
A 1.1-million-acre stretch of sandy forests and wetlands between Philadelphia and the Atlantic. Catch a glimpse of the rare Pine Barrens Tree Frog; hike, fish, camp, and kayak at the first U.S. National Reserve, established in 1978; visit Batsto, an 1880s glass and iron company town; wander the country's largest pygmy pine forest, near Chatsworth.

Winterthur Garden and Museum
Route 52 in Delaware's Brandywine Valley, 30 miles southwest of Philadelpha
800-448-3883
www.winterthur.org
Former home of horticulturist and antique collector Henry Francis du Pont, Winterthur is a haven for travelers interested in either. The mansion displays antiques as well as decorative and functional objects representing Americana back to the 17th century. There's something blooming on the thousand-acre grounds from January through November. Children love getting lost in the Enchanted Woods.

About the Author

JOHN M. THOMPSON has written nine National Geographic Books including, most recently, *Wildlands of the Upper South* and *The Western Edge*. He is a contributor to the *Almanac of American History* and is at work on a book called *National Park Tours with Rangers*, also both published by National Geographic. In the past his focus has been on the southeastern United States, but his knowledge and interests have recently broadened to include other regions of the continental U.S. He lives in Charlottesville, Virginia, and travels as often as he can.

Acknowledgments

Material used in this book first appeared in the following National Geographic Books:
National Geographic Guide to America's Hidden Corners (1998)
National Geographic Guide to Small Town Escapes (2000)
National Geographic Guide to Weekend Getaways: 74 Mini-Vacations Across America (2002)

Illustrations Credits

1, Stephen L. Alvarez; 2, Jim Richardson/ CORBIS; 4, New Orleans Metropolitan Convention and Visitors Bureau, Inc.; 10, Craig Aurness/ CORBIS; 12, Stuart Westmorland/ CORBIS; 15, David Conklin; 16, Craig Tuttle/ CORBIS; 18, CORBIS; 20-21, Jim Richardson; 23, Mark Larson; 25, Sarah Leen; 27, Steve Casimiro/The Image Bank/Getty Images; 28, Larry Ulrich; 29, Peter Essick; 30, Istockphoto.com/irish blue; 32-33, Geoffrey Clifford/Getty Images; 34, Monterey Bay Aquarium Foundation/Ken Bach; 35, Monterey Bay Aquarium Foundation; 36 (Left), Robert Dalton/istockphoto.com; 36 (Right), ML Sinibaldi/ CORBIS; 37 (Left), John Elk III, 37 (Right), Phil Schermeister; 38-39, Diane Cooke; 40, Jack Dykinga; 43, Luc Beziat/Getty Images; 44-45, Maria Stenzel; 46, Kelly Rigby; 48, Michael DeYoung/ CORBIS; 50, Bettman/ CORBIS; 53 (Top), Bill Haas; 53 (Bottom), Circle Z Ranch; 54-55, Bill Haas; 57, Nicholas DeVore III /Network Aspen; 58, Eric Lars Bakke; 59, Eric Lars Bakke; 61, Chris Johns; 62, Jan Butchofsky/ CORBIS; 64 (Top), Phil Schermeister; 64 (Bottom), David Muench; 65 (Left), David Muench; 65(Right), Tony Demin/Network Aspen; 66-67, Laurence Parent; 68, Philip Gould; 71, Lee Foster/AGPix; 72-73, SACVB/Al Rendon; 74, Donovan Reese /Getty Images; 76, East Texas Oil Museum; 79 (Top), New Orleans Metropolitan Convention and Visitors Bureau, Inc./Ann Purcell, (Bottom), New Orleans Metropolitan Convention and Visitors Bureau, Inc./Romney Caruso; 80, Charles O'Rear/ CORBIS; 82-83, David Bishop; 85, John Wilding; 86, Tom Porter; 88 (Top), New Orleans Metropolitan Convention and Visitors Bureau/Richard Nowitz; 88 (Bottom), Joseph McNally/Getty Images; 89 (Left), Jim Argo; 89 (Right), Jonathan Wallen; 90-91, Fred Hirschmann; 92, AGPix/Greg Ryan/ Sally Beyer; 95, Historical Picture Archive/ CORBIS; 96, James L. Stanfield; 97, Phil Schermeister/ CORBIS; 99, Fred J. Maroon/Folio; 100-101, Amana Colonies Convention and Visitors Bureau; 103, Getty Images; 104-105, Sandy Felsenthal/ CORBIS; 106, Sandy Felsenthal/ CORBIS;108, James L. Amos; 109 Everett Johnson/Folio; 110, Clay Perry/ CORBIS; 112-113, AGPix/Danita Delimont; 114, Daniel Grogan; 116 (Top), Leslie Kelly; 116 (Bottom), Hank Erdmann; 117 (Left), John E. Rees; 117 (Right), Sam Abell; 118 Richard Bickel/ CORBIS; 120, Maggie Steber; 123, James Randklev/ CORBIS; 124, Richard Bickel/ CORBIS; 127, Crystal Coast Tourism Development Authority; 128-129, Mike Booher/TRANSPARENCIES, Inc.; 130, Beaufort Historical Association; 131, Tom Raymond; 132-133, Peter Montanti/ Mountain Photographics, Inc.; 135, Courtesy Memphis Convention & Visitors Bureau; 136, Michael Nichols; 137, Gail Mooney; 138, Bob Guthridge; 140-141, O'Neil Arnold; 143, Kelly/Mooney Photography; 144 (Left), Connie Toops; 144 (Right), Kelly Culpepper/TRANSPARENCIES, Inc.; 145 (Left), Virginia Tourism Corporation; 145 (Right), Linda Bailey/Earth Scenes; 146-147, Phil Schermeister; 148, Kelly-Mooney Photography/ CORBIS; 151, Phil Schermeister; 152-153, Jeremy Woodhouse; 154, Jim McElholm/Single Source Photography; 156, Bettman/ CORBIS; 158-159, Edith Wharton Restorations, Inc.; 161 (Top), Berkshire Visitors Bureau/ A. Blake Garnder; 161 (Bottom), Kelly-Mooney Photography/ CORBIS; 163, Ralph Pugliese, Jr.; 164, Ralph Pugliese, Jr.; 165, Courtesy Bedell Cellars; 166, Harold Corsini/Courtesy Western Pennsylvania Conservancy; 168, Bob Krist; 170, Kelly/Mooney Photography/CORBIS; 172, Bucks County Conference and Visitors Bureau; 173, Gail Mooney; 174 (Left), William Johnson/Stock Boston; 174 (Right), Dick Swanson; 175 (Left), Gail Mooney; 175 (Right), Alan & Linda Detrick; 176, Phil Schermeister; 179, Bill Haas; 181, New Orleans Metropolitan Convention and Visitors Bureau, Inc.; 183, William van Overbeek; 185, Courtesy Memphis Convention & Visitors Bureau; 187, Bucks County Conference & Visitors Bureau.

Index

Boldface indicates illustrations.

Abilene, Kans. **89**, 90
Abingdon, Va. 145, **145**
Adam Puchta Winery, Hermann, Mo. 84
Adams, Mount, Wash. 18–19
Adirondack Park, N.Y. 174
Adler, Dankmar 106
Admiralty Inlet, Wash. 14
Akeley, Minn. **97**
The Alamo, San Antonio, Tex. 70
Albuquerque, N.M. 64
Alcatraz, Calif. 37
Alder Gulch, Mont. 63
Amana Colonies, Iowa 98–99, **100–101**, 102
American bison **91**
American Fur Company, Mackinac
    Island, Mich. 111
American River, Calif. 37
Amish Community, Berlin, Ohio **110**,
    111, **112–114**, 114–115
Andreas Canyon, Calif. 30
Anza-Borrego Desert State Park, Calif.
    26, **27–28**
Apalachicola Coast, Fla. **118–119, 124**,
    125–126
Aquarius Plateau, Utah 51
Arikara Indians 96
Arizona *see* Western states
Arizona Strip 51–52
Arkansas *see* South-central states
Arkansas River, Colo. 58
Astor, John Jacob 111
Astoria, Oreg. 23–24
Audubon National Wildlife Refuge, N.
    Dak. 96
Augusta, Mo. 84
Ballet Folklorico de San Antonio **74**
Bandera, Tex. 88
Bannack, Mont. 63
Barter Theatre, Abingdon, Va. 145, **145**
Beale Street, Memphis, Tenn. **137**, 139
Beaufort, N.C. **1**, 126, **127–130**, 130–131
Beauregard-Keyes House, New Orleans,
    La. 78
Bell, Josiah 130
Bemidji, Minn. 96, 98
Berea, Ky. 139, **140–141**, 142, **143**
Berea College, Ky. **140–141**, 142, **143**
Berkshires, Mass. **148**, 157, **158–159**, 160,
    161
Berlin, Ohio **110**, 111, **112–114**, 114–115
Big Hole Valley, Mont. 60–61
Big Thicket National Preserve, Tex.
    66–67, 75
Bighorn Mountains, Wyo. 65
Bingham, William 150
Binion's Horseshoe, Las Vegas, Nev. 46–47
Bitterroot Mountains, Mont. 61, **61**
Bivalve, N.J. **174**
Black Canyon of the Gunnison National
    Park, Colo. 65, **65**
Blue Belle Saloon, Guthrie, Okla. 90
Bodmer, Karl 94–95, **95**
Boone, Daniel 134
Boone Tavern Hotel, Berea, Ky. **143**
Borrego Badlands, Calif. 26
Boulder Mountain, Utah 47, 51

Bourbon Street , New Orleans, La. 78
Bowie, Jim 70
Bowman's Hill Wildflower Preserve, Pa. 173
Boyd & Wurthman Restaurant, Berlin,
    Ohio 115
Braddock, Maj. Gen. Edward 167
Brandywine Valley, Pa. 175, **175**
Breakwater Hotel, Miami, Fla. 123
Breweries, Denver, Colo. 65, **65**
Buck, Pearl S. 172-173
Bucks County, Pa. **170**, 169–173, **172, 173**
Buena Vista, Colo. **58**, 60
Bunyan, Paul **97**, 98
Burnham & Root 106
Burns, Oreg. 25
Burr Trail Road, Utah 51
Butte, Mont. 63
Caddo Lake State Park, Jefferson, Tex. 75
Caddoan Mounds State Historical Park,
    Tex. 77
Café du Monde, New Orleans, La. 78
California *see* Pacific Coast
Cannery Row, Monterey, Calif. 31
Cap San Blas, Apalachicola, Fla. 126
Cape Lookout State Park, Oreg. 22
Carmel, Calif. 34
Carrot Island, Beaufort, N.C. 131
Casa Casuarina, Miami, Fla. 123
Cascades, Wash. 18–19
Cassoday, Kans. 87
Cather, Willa 116
Cavalier Hotel, Miami, Fla. 123
Chalk Creek, Colo. 60
Charbonneau, Toussaint 95–96
Chase County Courthouse, Cottonwood
    Falls, Kans. **86**, 87
Cheney House B&B, Chicago, Ill. 107
Chester County, Pa. **175**
Chester Inn, Jonesborough, Tenn. 134
Chicago, Ill. 102, **103–106**, 106–107
Cholla Cactus Garden, Calif. **29**
Circle Z Ranch, Patagonia, Ariz. 53
Clark, William 94
Clatsop Spit, Oreg. 24
Clay, Cassius 142
Cliff House, San Francisco, Calif. 36
Coachella Valley, Calif. 30
Coconut Grove, Miami, Fla. 124
Coit Tower, San Francisco, Calif. 36
Cold Spring, N.Y. 175
Colorado *see* Western states
Colorado Desert, Calif. 26
Colorado Rockies 56–57, **57–59**, 60
Columbia, Calif. 37
Columbia River, Oreg. 23–24
Columbus, Ind. 116
Constitution, Mount, Wash. 36
Coors, Adolph 65
Coral Gables, Miami, Fla. 124–125
Corchaug Indians 163
Coree Indians 130
Corey Creek Vineyard, Cutchogue, N.Y. 165
Cottonwood Falls, Kans. **86**, 87
Cottonwood Hot Springs and Spa, Buena
    Vista, Colo. 60
Council Grove, Kans. 87
Cranberry Thistle, Jonesborough, Tenn. 135

Crane, Oreg. 26
Crockett, Davy 70, 134
Cross Ranch State Park, N. Dak. 94
Cumberland, Ga. 144
Cunanan, Andrew 123
Custom House, Monterey, Calif. 31
Cutchogue, N.Y. **162**, 163, **164–165**,
    166–167
Cuttyhunk Island, Mass. 174, **174**
Dartmouth College, Hanover , N.H. **174**
De Garmo Canyon, Oreg. 25
De Smet, S. Dak. 116, **116**
Deering, James 124
Denver, Colo. 65, **65**
Der Bake Oven, Berlin, Ohio 115
Diamond, Oreg. 26
Dinosaur National Monument, Utah 65
Donaldsonville, La. 88
Door Peninsula, Wis. 117
Doylestown, Pa. **168**, 169
Dutton, Clarence 47
Eagle Harbor, Ephraim, Wis. **116**
East Texas *see* South-central states
East Texas Oil Museum, Kilgore, Tex. **76**, 77
Edward Ball Wakulla Springs State Park,
    Apalachicola, Fla. 126
Eisenhower, Dwight D. 90
El Dorado County, Calif. 37
El Mercado, San Antonio, Tex. 71, **74**
Elbert, Mount, Colo. 57, 60
Elvis Presley Boulevard, Memphis, Tenn.
    139
Ephraim, Wis. **116**, 117
Escalante, Utah **38–40, 46, 47, 48–49**, 51
Eureka Springs, Ark. 78, **80, 81**
Excelsior Hotel, Jefferson, Tex. 75
Fairmont Hotel, San Francisco, Calif. 36
Fallingwater, Laurel Highlands, Pa. **166**,
    167, 169
Farmers Market Plaza, San Antonio, Tex. **74**
Father of Waters 93–94
Faulkner, William 144
Fisherman's Wharf, Monterey, Calif. 31
Flint Hills, Kans. 85, **86**, 87
Florida *see* Southern states
Fonthill, Doylestown, Pa. 169–172, **173**
Fort Berthold Indian Res., N. Dak. 96
Fort Bragg, Calif. 37
Fort Clark, N. Dak. 94–95, **95**
Fort Mackinac, Mackinac Island, Mich. 111
Fort Mandan Historic Site, N. Dak. 94
Fort Necessity National Battlefield, Pa. 167
Fort Stevens State Park, Oreg. 24
Fort Worden State Park, Wash. 15, **16–17**
Frank Lloyd Wright Home and Studio,
    Chicago, Ill. 107
Fredonia, Ariz. 51
Fremont Street, Las Vegas, Nev. 46
French, Daniel Chester 160
French, Peter 25
French Quarter, New Orleans, La. 77–78
Frenchglen, Oreg. 26
Galena, Ill. 117, **117**
Gallier House, New Orleans, La. 78
Garrison Dam, N. Dak. 94
Garyville, La. 88
Georgia *see* Southern states

Gifford Pinchot National Forest, Wash. 19
Golden Gate Bridge, San Francisco, Calif. **36,** 37
The Good Earth (Buck) 171–173
Graceland, Memphis, Tenn. 138, 139
Grand Canyon National Park, Ariz. 51, 52
Grand Hotel, Mackinac Island, Mich. 107, **109**
Grand Staircase–Escalante National Monument, Utah **38–39,** 47, **48–49**
Grapevine Market and Café, Donaldsonville, La. 88
Great Chicago Fire (1871) 102
Great Swamp Fight, South County, R.I. 155
Greylock, Mount, Mass. 160
Gunnison National Park, Colo. 65, **65**
Guthrie, Okla. 88, **89,** 90
Hancock Shaker Village, Pittsfield, Mass. **161**
Hanover, N.H. 174, **174**
Harney County Historical Museum, Oreg. 25
Harshaw Creek, Ariz. 56
Hart Mountain National Antelope Refuge, Oreg. 25
Hawthorne, Nathaniel 157
Hays House Restaurant, Council Grove, Kans. 87
Hermann, Mo. 81, **82–83,** 84, **85**
Hermann-Grima Historic House, New Orleans, La. 78
Hermannhof Winery, Hermann, Mo. 84
Hickok, Wild Bill 90
Hidatsa Indians **95,** 96
Hill Country, Tex. 88, **88**
Holmes County, Ohio **112–113,** 114
Illinois *see* Midwestern states
Indiana *see* Midwestern states
Ingalls, Laura 116
Institute of Texan Cultures, San Antonio, Tex. 70
Intracoastal Waterway **1**
Iowa *see* Midwestern states
Iowa River Valley 99
Itasca State Park, Minn. 98
Jackson, Andrew 77, 134
Jackson Square, New Orleans, La. 77–78
James A. Michener Art Museum, Doylestown, Pa. 172
Jefferson, Tex. 75
John Hancock Center, Chicago, Ill. 107
Johnson, Andrew 134
Johnston Ridge Observatory, Wash. 19
Johnstown, Pa. 169
Jones, Robert Trent, Sr. 116
Jonesborough, Tenn. **131–133,** 134–135
Joshua Tree National Park, Calif. 26, **29,** 30
Kaibab National Forest, Ariz. 51, 52
Kaibab Paiute 52
Kaibab Plateau, Ariz. **50,** 52
Kansa Indians 87
Kansas *see* South-central states
Katahdin, Mount, Me. **152–153**
Katy Trail State Park, Mo. 84
Kaw Mission State Historic Site, Council Grove, Kans. 87
Kearney, Nebr. 116
Kentuck Knob, Laurel Highlands, Pa. 169
Kentucky *see* Southern states
Keys View, Calif. 30
Kilgore, Tex. **76,** 77
King, B.B. **138,** 139

Knife River Indian Villages National Historic Site, N. Dak. 95
Lake Erie Islands, Ohio 117, **117**
Lake Itasca, Minn. **92, 96,** 97–98
Lake Michigan, Chicago, Ill. 102, 107
Lake Sakakawea, N. Dak. 94
Las Vegas, Nev. 42–43, **43–45,** 46–47
Laurel Highlands, Pa. **166,** 166–167, 169
Leadville, Colo. 56–57, **57,** 60
Lebold-Vahsholtz House, Abilene, Kans. **89**
Lenox, Mass. **148, 158–159,** 160, **161**
Leslie Hotel, Miami, Fla. 123
Lewis, Meriwether 94
Lewis and Clark National Historical Park, Oreg. 23
Lewis and Clark territory, N. Dak. 94–96
Lighthouse Point, Santa Cruz, Calif. 31
Little House on the Prairie (Wilder) 116
Log House Craft Gallery, Berea, Ky. 142
Long Island Sound, N.Y. **162,** 163
Longwood Gardens, Chester County, Pa. 175
Louisiana *see* South-central states
Lower Death Hollow, Escalante, Utah **40**
Lufkin, Tex. 75
The Luxor, Las Vegas, Nev. 42–43, **44–45**
Mackinac Island, Mich. 107, **108–109,** 111
Maine *see* Northeastern states
Malheur National Wildlife Refuge, Oreg. **24,** 25
Mandan Indians 95, 96
Manhattan Building, Chicago, Ill. 106
Mardi Gras 79
Market Square, San Antonio, Tex. 71
Massachusetts *see* Northeastern states
Massive, Mount, Colo. 57
Maximilian, Prince 95
Melville, Herman 157
Memphis, Tenn. **135–138,** 138–139
Mendocino, Calif. 37, **37**
Mercer, Henry 171–172
Mercer Museum, Doylestown, Pa. **168**
Metz, Christian 99
Mi Tierra Café and Bakery, San Antonio, Tex. **71,** 74
Miami, Fla. **120,** 122–125
Miami Beach, Fla. 122, **123**
Michener, James A. 172
Michigan *see* Midwestern states
Midwestern states: Amana Colonies, Iowa **98–99, 100–101,** 102; Berlin, Ohio **110,** 111, **112–114,** 114–115; Chicago, Ill. 102, **103–106,** 106–107; Columbus, Ind. 116; De Smet, S. Dak. 116, **116;** Ephraim, Wis. 116, 117; Galena, Ill. 117, **117;** Lake Erie Islands, Ohio 117, **117;** Lewis and Clark territory, N. Dak. 94–96; Mackinac Island, Mich. 107, **108–109,** 111; Mississippi River headwaters, Minn. **92, 96,** 96–98; Platte River, Nebr. 116
Minatarre Indians **95**
Minnesota *see* Midwestern states
Mission of the Pueblo of Laguna 64
Mission San Xavier del Bac, Ariz. **54–55**
Mississippi *See* Southern states
Mississippi Palisades State Park, Galena, Ill. 117
Mississippi River headwaters, **92, 96,** 96–98
Missouri *see* South-central states

Missouri-Kansas-Texas Railroad 84
Mix, Tom 90
Mojave Desert, Calif. 26
Monadnock Building, Chicago, Ill. 106
Monarch Crest Scenic Tramway, Colo. 60
Monongahela National Forest, W. Va. 145, **145**
Montana *see* Western states
Monterey, Calif. 31, **32–33**
Monterey Bay, Calif. 31, **32–33,** 34
Monterey Bay Aquarium, Calif. 34, **35**
Monterey Submarine Canyon, Calif. 31
Moon Walk, New Orleans, La. 77
Moosehead Lake Region, Me. 150–151, **151–153,** 154–155
Mosquito Range, Colo. 57
The Mount, Lenox, Mass. **158–159,** 160
Mount Pleasant Vineyards, Augusta, Mo. 84
Mount Princeton Hot Springs Resort, Buena Vista, Colo. 60
Mount Rainier National Park, Wash. **12,** 19
Mount Washington Tavern, Pa. 167
Murray Canyon, Calif. 30
Museum of Amana History, Iowa **99,** 102
Narada Falls, Wash. 22
Narragansett, R.I. 157
Narragansett Indians 155
Narrows Earth Trail, Calif. 26
Natchez Trace Parkway, Miss. **2–3,** 144
National Mining Hall of Fame & Museum, Leadville, Colo. 57, **57**
National Storytelling Festival, Jonesborough, Tenn. **131,** 134
Nebraska *see* Midwestern states
Nevada *see* Western states
New Bedford, Mass. 174
New Hampshire *see* Northeastern states
New Haven, Mo. 84
New Hope, Pa. 173
New Jersey *see* Northeastern states
New Mexico *see* Western states
New Orleans, La. **4,** 77–78, **79**
New York *see* Northeastern states
Nez Perce Indians 61
Nob Hill, San Francisco, Calif. 36
North American Museum of Ancient Life, Utah 64
North Carolina *see* Southern states
North Carolina Maritime Museum, Beaufort, N.C. 131
North Dakota *see* Midwestern states
Northeastern states: Adirondack Park, N.Y. 174; Berkshires, Mass. **148,** 157, **158–159,** 160, **161;** Brandywine Valley, Pa. 175, **175;** Bucks County, Pa. **170–173,** 169–173, **170,** 171, **171;** Cold Spring, N.Y. 175; Cutchogue, N.Y. **162,** 163, **164–165,** 166–167; Cuttyhunk Island, Mass. 174, **174;** Hanover, N.H. 174, **174;** Laurel Highlands, Pa. **166,** 166–167, 169; Moosehead Lake Region, Me. 150–151, **151–153,** 154–155; New Jersey coast 175, **175;** South County, R.I. **154,** 155, **156,** 157
Nottoway Plantation, White Castle, La. 88
Oak Alley Plantation, La. **68**
Oak Park, Chicago, Ill. 107
Ocean Drive, Miami, Fla. 122–123
Ohio *see* Midwestern states

Ohiopyle, Pa. 169
Ojibwa Indians 97, 107
Okefenokee Swamp, Ga. 144, **144**
Oklahoma *see* South-central states
Old Burying Ground, Beaufort, N.C. 130
The Old House, Cutchogue, N.Y. **164,** 166
Old Narragansett Church, Wickford, R.I. 157
Orcas Island, Wash. 36, **36**
Oregon: coast 22, **23,** 23–24; high desert
    24, 24–26
Osage Indians 87
Ottawa County, Ohio 117
Ozark Mountains, Ark. 78–79, 81
Ozawindeb Indians 97
Pacific Coast: El Dorado County, Calif.
    37; Mendocino, Calif. 37;
    Monterey Bay, Calif. 31, **32–33,**
    34, **35**; Orcas Island, Wash. 36,
    36; Oregon coast 22, **23,** 23–24;
    Oregon high desert **24,** 24–26;
    Port Townsend, Wash. 13–15,
    15, 16**–**17; San Diego back-
    country 26, **27–29,** 30; San
    Francisco, Calif. **36,** 36–37;
    Volcano Trail, Wash. **18,** 18–19,
    20–21, 22
Paiute Indians 50
Palm Springs, Calif. 26, 30
Park Rapids, Minn. 96
Patagonia, Ariz. 52, **53–55,** 56
Pearl S. Buck House and Historic Site,
    Bucks County, Pa. 172–173
Pebble Beach, Calif. 34, **10–11**
Pei, I. M. 116
Pennsylvania *see* Northeastern states
Pete French Round Barn State Heritage
    Site, Oreg. 25
Peter Iredale (shipwreck) 24
Phillips, Sam 139
Piney Woods, Tex. 75
Pipe Spring National Monument, Ariz. 52
Pittsfield, Mass. **161**
Placerville, Calif. 37
Platte River, Nebr. 116
Point Wilson Lighthouse, Wash. **16–17**
Port Townsend, Wash. 13–15, **15,** 16**–**17
Powell, John Wesley 47
Preservation Hall, New Orleans, La. 78
Presley, Elvis **135–136,** 138, 139
Pueblo country, N.M. 64, **64**
Puget Sound, Wash. 36
Put-in-Bay, Ohio **117**
Queen Anne's Revenge (ship) 131
Rainbow Trail, Colo. 60
Rainier, Mount, Wash. 19, 22
Rancho Mirage, Calif. 26
Rauch Vineyard, Hermann, Mo. **82–83**
Red Fleet State Park, Vernal, Utah 64–65
Red Lion Inn, Stockbridge, Mass. 160
Rees-Hawley House, Jonesborough, Tenn.
    132–133, 134–135
Rhode Island *see* Northeastern states
River Road African American Museum,
    Sorrento, La. 88
River Walk, San Antonio, Tex. 71, **72–73**
Robller Vineyard, New Haven, Mo. 84
Rockwell, Norman 160
Rookery Building, Chicago, Ill. **104–105,** 106
Rusk County, Tex. 77
Saarinen, Eliel 116
St. George Island State Park,
    Apalachicola, Fla. 126

St. Helens, Baron (England) 19
St. Joseph Peninsula State Park,
    Apalachicola , Fla. 126
St. Louis Cathedral, New Orleans, La. 77
St. Marks National Wildlife Refuge,
    Apalachicola, Fla. 126
St. Marys, Ga. 144
St. Vincent Island, Fla. 118–119
Salida, Colo. **58,** 60
Salton Sea, Calif. 30
San Andreas Fault, Calif. 30
San Antonio, Tex. 70–71, **71–74,** 74
San Diego backcountry, Calif. 26, **27–30,** 30
San Francisco, Calif. **36,** 36–37
San Francisco Plantation, Garyville, La. 88
San Gorgonio Mountain, Calif. 30
San Jacinto, Mount, Calif. 30
San Juans, Wash. 36
Sangre de Cristo Mountains, N.M. 64
Santa Cruz, Calif. **30,** 31
Santa Fe Trail 87
Santa Rita Mountains, Ariz. 52, 56
Sawatch Range, Colo. 56–57
Scarborough State Beach, R.I. 157
Schoolcraft, Henry 97–98
Schrock's Amish Farm, Berlin, Ohio 115
Sculpture Park, Salida, Colo. **58**
Seal Rocks, San Francisco, Calif. 36
Sears Tower, Chicago, Ill. **103,** 107
Seaside, Oreg. **23**
Shackleford Banks, Beaufort, N.C. 131
Sharpe's Creek Drive, Kans. 87
Sheridan, Wyo. 65
Sinatra, Frank 42
Smith, Richard 155
Smith's Castle, South County, R.I. 155
Sonoita Creek, Ariz. **53,** 56
Sonoita Valley, Ariz. 52
Sorrento, La. 88
South Beach, Miami, Fla. **123**
South-central states: Abilene, Kans. **89,**
    90; antebellum plantation man-
    sions, La. 88, **88;** East Texas 75,
    76, 77; Eureka Springs, Ark. 78,
    80, 81; Flint Hills, Kans. 85, **86,**
    87; Guthrie, Okla. 88, **89,** 90;
    Missouri wine country 81,
    82–83, 84, **85;** New Orleans, La.
    77–78, **79;** San Antonio, Tex.
    70–71, **71–74,** 74; Texas Hill
    Country 88, **88**
South County, R.I. **154,** 155, **156,** 157
South Dakota *see* Midwestern states
Southern Highland Craft Guild, N.C. 145
Southern Paiute Indians 50
Southern states: Abingdon, Va. 145, **145;**
    Apalachicola Coast, Fla.
    118**–**119, **124,** 125**–**126;
    Beaufort, N.C. 126, **127–130,**
    130–131; Berea, Ky. 139,
    140–141, 142; Cumberland, Ga.
    144; hills of Mississippi 144;
    Jonesborough, Tenn. **131–133,**
    134–135; Memphis, Tenn.
    135–138, 138**–**139; Miami, Fla.
    120, 122–125; Monongahela
    National Forest, W. Va. 145,
    145; Okefenokee Swamp, Ga.
    144, **144;** Southern Highland
    Crafts, N.C. 144, **144**
Spanish Governor's Palace, San Antonio,
    Tex. 74

Spouter Inn, Beaufort, N.C. 131
St. Helens, Mount, Wash. 19, **20–21**
Steamer Lane, Santa Cruz, Calif. 31
Steens Mountain, Oreg. 25
Steinbeck, John 31
Stockbridge, Mass. 158
Stone Hill Winery, Hermann, Mo. 84
The Strip, Las Vegas, Nev. 42–43, 42–46
Sullivan, Louis H. 106
Sun Studio, Memphis, Tenn. **135,** 139
Sunderland, Mass. **147**
Tahoma 19
Tallgrass Prairie National Preserve, Kans. 87
Tamalpais, Mount, Calif. 36
Tanglewood, Lenox, Mass. 160, **161**
Taos, N.M. 64, **64**
Telegraph Hill, San Francisco, Calif. 36
Tennessee *see* Southern states
Tennessee River Hills, Miss. 144
Texas *see* South-central states
Texas Forestry Museum, Lufkin, Tex. 75
Three Capes Scenic Drive, Oreg. 22–23
Tillamook, Oreg. 23
Top of the Mark, San Francisco, Calif. 36
Topeka, Kans. 87
Tudor Rose, Salida, Colo. 60
Tusayan, Ariz. 51
Ulysses S. Grant Home State Historic
    Site, Galena, Ill. 117
Unity Temple, Chicago, Ill. **106,** 107
University of California, Santa Cruz,
    Calif. 31
Utah 47, 51; *see also* Western states
Vancouver, George 19
The Venetian, Las Vegas, Nev. 43
Vernal, Utah 64–65
Vintage Restaurant, Hermann, Mo. 84
Virginia *see* Southern states
Virginia City, Mont. 62, 63
Vizcaya, Miami, Fla. 124
Volcano Trail, Wash. **18,** 18–19, **20–21,** 22
Washburn, N. Dak. 94
Washington *see* Pacific Coast
Washington, George 167
Washington Crossing Historic Park,
    Bucks County, Pa. **172**
West Coast *see* Pacific Coast
West Virginia *see* Southern states
Westerly, R.I. 157
Western states: Colorado Rockies 56–57,
    57–59, 60; Denver, Colo. 65, **65;**
    Escalante, Utah **46,** 47, **48–49,**
    51; Gunnison National Park,
    Colo. 65, **65;** Las Vegas, Nev.
    42–43, **43–45,** 46–47; Northern
    Arizona **50,** 51–52; Patagonia,
    Ariz. 52, **53–55,** 56; Pueblo
    country, N.M. 64, **64;** Sheridan,
    Wyo. 65; Southwest Montana
    60–61, **61–62,** 63; Taos, N.M.
    64, **64;** Vernal, Utah 64–65
Wharton, Edith 160
White Castle, La. **88**
Wickford, R.I. 155, 157
Wilder, Laura Ingalls 116
Williams, Roger 155
Wisconsin *see* Midwestern states
Wonderland Trail, Wash. 22
Wright, Frank Lloyd 106, 107, 166–167, 169
Wynkoop Brewing Co., Denver, Colo. 65, **65**
Wyoming *see* Western states
Yaquina Bay, Oreg. 22

American Journeys

Edited by John M. Thompson

Published by the National Geographic Society
John M. Fahey, Jr., President and Chief Executive Officer
Gilbert M. Grosvenor, Chairman of the Board
Nina D. Hoffman, Executive Vice President

Prepared by the Book Division
Kevin Mulroy, Senior Vice President and Publisher
Kristin Hanneman, Illustrations Director
Marianne R. Koszorus, Design Director
Barbara Brownell Grogan, Executive Editor

Staff for this Book
Susan Tyler Hitchcock, Project and Text Editor
Peggy Archambault, Art Director
Kay Hankins, Illustrations Editor
Susan Straight, Researcher
Margo Browning, Contributing Editor
Carl Mehler, Director of Maps
Nicholas P. Rosenbach, Map Researcher and Editor
Gregory Ugiansky, Map Production
R. Gary Colbert, Production Director
Lewis Bassford, Production Project Manager
Rachel Sweeney, Illustrations Specialist
Cataldo Perrone, Design Assistant
Suzanne Zito Slezak, Proofreader

Manufacturing and Quality Control
Christopher A. Liedel, Chief Financial Officer
Phillip L. Schlosser, Managing Director
John T. Dunn, Technical Director
Chris Brown, Manager

Founded in 1888, the National Geographic Society is one of the world's largest nonprofit scientific and educational organizations. Its mission is to increase and diffuse geographic knowledge while promoting conservation of the world's cultural and natural resources. National Geographic reflects the world through its five magazines, television programs, films, radio, books, videos, maps, interactive media and merchandise. National Geographic magazine, the Society's official journal, published in English and 27 local-language editions, is read by 40 million people each month in every country in the world. The National Geographic Channel reaches more than 260 million households in 27 languages in 160 countries. Nationalgeographic.com averages around 60 million page views per month. National Geographic has funded more than 8,000 scientific research projects and supports an education program combating geography illiteracy.

For more information,
log on to nationalgeographic.com;
AOL Keyword: NatGeo.

NATIONAL GEOGRAPHIC SOCIETY
1145 17th Street N.W.
Washington, D.C. 20036-4688 U.S.A.
Visit the Society's Web site at
www.nationalgeographic.com.

Library of Congress Cataloging-in-Publication Data
Thompson, John M. (John Milliken), 1959-
American journeys : weekends across the U.S. / by John M. Thompson.
  p.cm
Includes bibliographical references and index.
United States ---Guidebooks. 2. United States--Description and travel 3. United States--Pictorial works. I. Title.

> E158.T475 2006
> 917.304'931--dc22
>   2005054007

ISBN 07922-4177-0 (Regular)
ISBN 07922-4178-9 (Deluxe)